THE Girls WHO Dish!

debbie
enjoy our
offerings
and share with
good friends
Kerri

THE Girls WHO Dish!

TOP WOMEN CHEFS COOK THEIR BEST!

Karen Barnaby, Margaret Chisholm, Deb Connors,
Tamara Kourchenko, Mary Mackay, Caren McSherry-Valagao,
Glenys Morgan, and Lesley Stowe

Whitecap Books
Vancouver/Toronto

Whitecap Books
Vancouver / Toronto

Edited by Elaine Jones
Proofread by Elizabeth McLean
Cover photographs by Lionel Trudel
Back cover photograph taken at the Dubrulle International
    Culinary & Hotel Institute of Canada
Cover design by Tanya Lloyd
Interior design by Warren Clark

Printed and bound in Canada

Canadian Cataloguing in Publication Data

The girls who dish

> Includes index.
> ISBN 1-55110-717-1

> 1. Cookery. I. Barnaby, Karen.
TX715.6.G593 1998   641.5   C98-910656-X

The publisher acknowledges the support of the Canada Council and the Cultural Services Branch of the Government of British Columbia in making this publication possible. We acknowledge the financial support of the Government of Canada through the Book Publishing Industry Development Program for our publishing activities.

Contents

Salads

Soups

Entrées

Vegetables

Desserts

Foreword

When you discover eight superlative women chefs all under one cover, "dishing" out their luscious recipe secrets, you are in for a culinary grand performance.

Their credentials are impeccable. Cookbook authors, caterers, cooking school owners and teachers, specialty food store and restaurant owners, radio and television personalities—and that is only what they do in their professional lives! All of these extraordinary women are actively involved in the community with fund-raising activities for the arts and medical research. All this expertise and commitment in one cookbook inspires a standing ovation.

Women chefs have come a long way in the last quarter of this century. In the early seventies, when I first entered the culinary scene, professional women chefs were rare, as were cookbooks written by women. Julia Child was emerging as a strong influence on the international scene with her cookbooks and television show, simplifying French and European cuisine for the home cook to re-create. Restaurants, however, were primarily dominated by European-trained male chefs, who were not interested in having women as an equal part of their kitchen team. There were very few cooking schools for professional or amateur cooks, and they were reluctant to accept women in their programs.

In 1973, I opened the first cooking school in Vancouver for amateur cooks, and my *Chef on the Run* cookbook series soon followed.

When Anne Willan's La Varenne Cooking School opened in Paris in 1975, it was the first bilingual cooking school in the world. I took thirty-six excited students from my Vancouver classes for an eye-opening week of classical French cooking. Julia Child and Anne Willan were definitely our early role models.

At the same time the culinary world was expanding, and the opportunities for both men and women were opening up. The California style, using a fresh, organic approach, became an alternative to classic European cuisine. We were all rushing out to buy wild greens and using exotic cheeses and balsamic vinaigrettes to impress our guests. With the expansion of global communications and travel, native cuisines from countries around the world became widely available to both professional and home cooks.

Women chefs are continuing to break the traditional mold, and this is exemplified by the women in this book—The Girls Who Dish.

I'm looking forward to tackling their amazing signature dishes in my home kitchen. The first dishes on my must-try list include Gorgonzola and Pecan

Soufflés; Lamb Loin with Seared Potato, Arugula and Red Wine Vinaigrette; Winter Squash Soup with Apple Cider and Thyme; and for the grand finale, Valrhona Chocolate Bread Pudding with Crème Fraîche and Dried Cherry Port Sauce.

The Girls Who Dish contains a multitude of delicious, easy-to-follow recipes that will allow you to cook like a professional in your own home. It is destined to be a classic, and will make you a star cook—male or female!

—Diane Clement

Appetizers

Roasted Garden Corn & Pepper Salsa

Roasting the vegetables makes this very different from other salsas. The roasting heightens the flavour and gives an irresistible taste sensation to grilled chicken and meats.

Makes about 2 cups (475 mL)		Caren McSherry-Valagao
2	ears fresh corn, in the husk	2
2	large ancho chiles, soaked in hot water	2
2	cloves garlic, minced	2
1/2 tsp.	cumin	2.5 mL
1 cup	cooked black turtle beans	240 mL
1	red bell pepper	1
1	green bell pepper	1
1	jalapeño pepper	1
1	large white onion	1
1/2 cup	chopped fresh cilantro	120 mL
1/2 tsp.	cumin	2.5 mL
	sea salt and freshly ground black pepper to taste	

Peel the husks of the corn back just far enough to remove the silk, then replace the husk over the corn. Cover the cobs with water and let them soak for 10 minutes.

Heat a barbecue or grill to high, place the corn on the grill and close the lid. Roast for about 15 minutes, turning the corn every 6 minutes or so. If you like a dark roasted appearance, remove the husk for the last 2–3 minutes of grilling. Set aside to cool.

Remove the chiles from the water, squeeze out the excess water and chop them finely. Combine the chiles, garlic, cumin and black beans in a large bowl. Roast all the peppers on the grill, turning them until they are blackened on all sides. Cool and remove the charred skin and seeds. Cut into medium dice and add to the bowl. Finely dice the jalapeño and add to the bowl.

Cut the onion into eighths, making sure that you leave some core attached to each piece so the onion does not fall apart. Lightly brush with oil and grill until brown. Dice the onion and add it to the bowl. Shuck the corn and add it to the bowl. Add the cilantro, cumin, salt and pepper and stir to combine.

Penne with Gorgonzola & Caramelized Onions

Serve this rich-tasting pasta in a small portion as an appetizer or for lunch with a green salad. Wash it down with some cool and crisp Italian white wine. Any blue cheese will do, though Gorgonzola has a richness that works especially well.

Serves 6		Margaret Chisholm
2 Tbsp.	unsalted butter	30 mL
1 1/2 lbs.	onions, very thinly sliced, about 6 cups (1.5 L)	680 g
	salt and freshly ground black pepper to taste	
1/2 cup	white wine	120 mL
2 Tbsp.	chopped parsley, preferably Italian parsley	30 mL
1 Tbsp.	salt, heaping	15 mL
1 lb.	dried penne pasta	454 g
1/2 cup	crumbled Gorgonzola cheese	120 mL

Melt the butter over medium-low heat in a medium saucepan and add the onions. Cover and cook for 1 hour or so, watching carefully to avoid browning and stirring occasionally. Remove the cover and turn the heat up to medium-high. Cook and stir until the onions are coloured a medium gold. Add generous grindings of pepper and season well with salt. Add the wine and cook over high heat until reduced to a glaze. Add the parsley. Set aside and keep warm.

Bring a large pot of water to a boil. Add the salt and pasta to the boiling water. Cook, stirring occasionally, until the pasta is tender but still firm to the bite, 9–11 minutes. Drain the pasta and return to the pot. Toss with the onions. Transfer to a heated serving bowl. Stir in the cheese and serve immediately.

Polenta Crostini with Mascarpone & Sun-Dried Tomato Pesto

Mascarpone is available in the freezer section of most large grocery stores or Italian delis. In a pinch you could substitute cream cheese, but it is worth the effort hunting out the real thing. The pesto will keep for up to two weeks in the refrigerator or several months in the freezer. It is great with pasta or mixed with a sandwich filling, such as tuna or chicken.

Makes 3 dozen		Lesley Stowe
4 cups	water	950 mL
1 1/2 tsp.	salt	7.5 mL
2 Tbsp.	olive oil	30 mL
2 cups + 2 Tbsp.	cornmeal	475 mL + 30 mL
2 Tbsp.	mascarpone	30 mL
2 Tbsp.	minced fresh herbs	30 mL
	salt and black pepper to taste	
1/4 cup	mascarpone	60 mL
1 recipe	Sun-Dried Tomato Pesto	1 recipe

Bring the water to a boil. Add the salt and olive oil. Slowly pour the cornmeal into the water in a steady stream. Cook over medium heat, stirring constantly, for about 15 minutes. Add the 2 Tbsp. (30 mL) mascarpone and the herbs. Season to taste.

Pour the polenta onto an 11- × 15-inch (28- × 38-cm) oiled baking sheet. Spread to 1/3-inch (.9-cm) thickness. Refrigerate. When cold, cut into shapes and grill or fry. To serve, top each piece with 1 tsp. (5 mL) mascarpone and a dab of Sun-Dried Tomato Pesto.

Sun-Dried Tomato Pesto

Makes 2 1/2 cups (600 mL)

2 cups	sun-dried tomatoes	475 mL
5	cloves garlic	5
2/3 cup	Parmesan cheese, grated	160 mL
3/4 cup	sun-dried tomato oil	180 mL

Drain the tomatoes, reserving the oil. Blend the tomatoes, garlic and cheese in a food processor until smooth. Add oil until the mixture is a good spreading consistency.

Tapenade

Tapenade is a Provençal olive paste, very popular in the south of France. Spread it on fresh baguettes and enjoy it with a glass of crisp, fruity white wine, or use it to stuff chicken breasts.

Makes about 1 1/2 cups (360 mL)   Caren McSherry-Valagao

1	head garlic, roasted (see page 7)	1
1 cup	Greek or niçoise olives, pitted	240 mL
2 Tbsp.	capers	30 mL
2–3	anchovy fillets	2–3
1 tsp.	fresh thyme, chopped	5 mL
2 Tbsp.	dark rum	30 mL
4 Tbsp.	extra-virgin olive oil	60 mL
1/2 tsp.	ground pepper	2.5 mL

Remove the papery skin from the garlic cloves. Place the garlic, olives, capers, anchovy and thyme in the bowl of a food processor. Pulse about 10–15 times until it is chunky. Add the rum and olive oil and pulse it a few more times. Do not completely purée it. Add the pepper.

Store in clean jars covered with a layer of olive oil. Chill until ready to use.

Double Tomato Bruschetta

For a bite of sunshine anytime, give the always available Roma a boost in flavour from its sun-dried cousin. Roasted garlic adds another sweet layer. Choose tomatoes with the most colour and a softer feel, but choose the firmest garlic bulb of the bunch. Add slivers of olive if desired or blend with chèvre or cream cheese. Always serve at room temperature.

Makes about 2 cups (475 mL)		Glenys Morgan
8–10	Roma tomatoes, cored and chopped	8–10
1/2 cup	sun-dried tomatoes, rehydrated or oil-pack, cut into fine strips	120 mL
1	head roasted garlic (see page 7)	1
1 Tbsp.	dried basil leaves	15 mL
2–3 Tbsp.	extra-virgin or fruity olive oil	30–45 mL
2–3 Tbsp.	balsamic or good-quality red wine vinegar salt and freshly ground black pepper to taste	30–45 mL
1	bunch fresh basil, leaves only	1
1	baguette	1

In a non-reactive bowl, combine the fresh and sun-dried tomatoes. Remove the cloves of garlic from the bulb with a knife tip or squeeze the garlic from the husk. Stir into the tomatoes and add the dried basil with 1–2 Tbsp. (15–30 mL) each of the olive oil and vinegar. Season with salt and pepper. Let the mixture rest for several minutes to allow the juices and flavours to blend.

Taste and adjust the flavours. If it's too acidic, add a little more oil. More vinegar will increase tanginess. At this point you can store it for one week. To keep the fresh basil from darkening, it should be added just before serving. Stack and roll the basil leaves like a cigar. Use a sharp knife to cut across the roll, making very fine strips called chiffonade. Add the basil to the mixture.

To toast the baguette, preheat the oven to 400°F (200°C). Cut the bread into 1/4-inch-thick (.6-cm) slices. Cutting on the diagonal creates an attractive elongated shape. Brush one side of each slice lightly with oil. Toast on a baking sheet in a single layer. For a crunchy version, toast both sides. The edges should be golden. For a more interesting flavour, grill the bread. Spread the baguette slices with the tomato mixture.

Roasted Garlic

Preheat the oven to 350°F (175°C). Make a straight cut, about 1/4 inch (.6 cm) deep, across the stem end of the garlic bulb, exposing the cloves. Rub the bulb with olive oil and pour a little oil in the centre of a piece of foil. Place the garlic cut side down on the foil. Wrap the foil around the bulb. Roast for 1 hour. Don't be tempted to speed the process by raising the oven temperature—it will often result in bitter garlic. Different types of garlic from different growing regions take varying amounts of time, but it generally takes at least an hour for the sugar in the garlic to develop, giving it the characteristic mellow flavour. When it's done, it should be caramel-coloured and soft in texture. If not, return it to the oven for another 15 minutes. Let the garlic cool in the foil. Remove the cloves with a knife tip or squeeze them out of the papery husks.

Confit & Cambozola

You've heard of duck confit. Well, this is a tomato confit. A whole roasted tomato, spiked with garlic, roasted in olive oil and basil, and topped with melting Cambozola cheese. This soft cheese, available in your local grocery store, is a cross of Brie and blue cheese. Smear this confit on sourdough baguette.

Serves 4		Mary Mackay
4	ripe tomatoes, core removed	4
20	cloves garlic, peeled	20
4 tsp.	finely chopped fresh basil	20 mL
4 Tbsp.	olive oil	60 mL
	salt to taste	
2 oz.	Cambozola cheese, sliced into 4 pieces	57 g
	cracked black pepper to taste	

Preheat the oven to 375°F (190°C). Slice about 1/8 inch (.3 cm) off the tops of the tomatoes. Place the tomatoes cut side up into 4 ramekins. The tomatoes should fit snugly. Press 5 garlic cloves into each tomato and sprinkle 1 tsp. (5 mL) chopped basil over top. Drizzle each with 1 tablespoon (15 mL) oil and season with salt. Place the ramekins on a baking sheet and bake on the middle rack for 75 to 90 minutes. To check for doneness, pierce the garlic cloves with the tip of a paring knife; the garlic should be soft. Remove from the oven and top each tomato with a slice of cheese. Season with lots of cracked black pepper.

Quesadillas with Shrimp & Avocado Relish

A light meal, perfect party food. Make it ahead and it can be quickly finished. The quesadillas should be thin and crisp. You can add sour cream and tomato salsa as garnishes.

Serves 4		Deb Connors
4	8-inch (20-cm) flour tortillas	4
8 oz.	spinach leaves, cleaned and trimmed	225 g
12 oz.	grated Monterey Jack cheese	340 g
2	Roma tomatoes, cut into fine dice	2
8 oz.	fresh shrimp	225 g
2	avocados, cut into fine dice	2
1 tsp.	fresh lime juice	5 mL
2 Tbsp.	finely diced red bell pepper	30 mL
2 Tbsp.	finely diced yellow bell pepper	30 mL
1/2	jalapeño pepper, seeded and cut into fine dice	1/2
2 Tbsp.	finely diced red onion	30 mL
1 Tbsp.	chopped cilantro	15 mL
3 Tbsp.	olive oil	45 mL
	salt and freshly ground black pepper to taste	
	hot pepper sauce to taste	

Place the tortillas on a flat surface. Place 1/4 of the spinach leaves on half of each tortilla. Distribute 1/4 of the cheese, tomato and shrimp over the spinach on each tortilla. Fold the tortillas in half (do not press). Lightly cover them with plastic wrap and refrigerate.

To make the avocado relish, toss together the diced avocado and lime juice. Stir in the peppers, red onion and cilantro. Add 1 Tbsp. (15 mL) of the olive oil and stir. Season with salt, pepper and hot sauce. Preheat the oven to 225°F (105°C).

Heat a small amount of the remaining olive oil in a non-stick pan. Cook one quesadilla over medium-low heat until crisp and golden on both sides. Keep warm in the oven while you continue cooking the quesadillas, using a small amount of olive oil for each one.

Slice each quesadilla in 3 pieces. Serve with the avocado relish on the side.

Roasted Garlic & Onion Flan

This is a great custard, because it's so versatile. I have served it as an appetizer with grilled or toasted bread, as a first course with a salad tossed with balsamic vinaigrette or as an accompaniment to roasted rack of lamb. The possibilities are endless.

Serves 6		Tamara Kourchenko
1	head garlic, roasted (see page 7)	1
2 Tbsp.	vegetable oil	30 mL
2 cups	onions, sliced very thin	475 mL
	salt and black pepper to taste	
7	large egg yolks	7
2 cups	whipping cream	475 mL
1 tsp.	chopped rosemary	5 mL
	salt and black pepper to taste	

Roast the garlic and when it is cool, squeeze the cloves out of the skins. You need 1 Tbsp. (15 mL) of garlic purée. Lower the oven temperature to 300°F (150°C).

Heat the oil in a large frying pan. When it is almost smoking, add the onions and stir so they don't burn. Lower the heat and cook slowly, stirring occasionally, until the onions are very soft and turn caramel brown, about 25 minutes. If the onions start to stick, lower the heat and sprinkle some water on them. Season with salt and pepper. Cool.

Whisk the egg yolks in a large bowl, then add the whipping cream, rosemary, 1 Tbsp. (15 mL) of garlic purée and the cooked onions. Season with salt and pepper.

Divide the mixture into six 3/4-cup (180-mL) buttered ramekins. Place the ramekins in an ovenproof pan and put it in the oven. Fill the pan with hot water so it comes halfway up the ramekins. Bake for about 1 hour, or until they feel firm. Refrigerate for several hours or overnight. Before serving, run a small, sharp knife around the edges of the ramekins and turn over to unmold. Serve either at room temperature or rewarm slightly, depending on what you are using them for.

Bambino Focaccia

*These savoury prosciutto, tomato and sage focaccias are great
party finger food—no forks or knives required. For a vegetarian
version, omit the prosciutto and use basil instead of sage.*

Makes 10 individual portions		Mary Mackay
1/2 cup	water at room temperature	120 mL
1/8 tsp.	dry yeast	.5 mL
1/2 cup	bread flour	120 mL
1 1/8 cups	water at room temperature	270 mL
1/4 cup	olive oil	60 mL
1 1/2 tsp.	salt	7.5 mL
1/2 tsp.	sugar	2.5 mL
1/2 tsp.	dry yeast	2.5 mL
3 cups	bread flour	720 mL
2 cups	mixed baby lettuce	475 mL
4	Roma tomatoes, cut into 8 wedges each	4
3 oz.	prosciutto, chopped	85 g
16	fresh sage leaves, shredded	16
5 oz.	mozzarella cheese, grated	140 g
	cracked black pepper to taste	

Make a sponge by hand-mixing the 1/2 cup (120 mL) water, 1/8 tsp. (.5 mL)
yeast and 1/2 cup (120 mL) bread flour in a small mixing bowl. Cover with a
tea towel and leave at room temperature for at least 8 hours, or up to 24 hours.

In a large mixing bowl, hand-mix the prepared sponge with the water and olive
oil. Add the salt, sugar, 1/2 tsp. (2.5 mL) yeast and 3 cups (720 mL) bread flour;
mix until the dough comes together. Turn onto a lightly floured surface and
knead for 10 to 15 minutes, until smooth. Return the dough to the mixing bowl
and cover with a tea towel. Let sit for 90 minutes at room temperature.

Divide the dough into 16 equal portions. Roll each piece into a 1/2-inch-thick
(1.2-cm) circle. Place on 2 oiled baking sheets, 8 pieces per sheet. Brush the tops
with olive oil and loosely cover with plastic wrap. Let the dough rise in a warm
area for 45 minutes.

Preheat the oven to 450°F (230°C). Place a baking sheet on the bottom of the
oven to heat. Poke holes into the dough with your fingers. Divide the mixed
baby lettuce, tomato wedges and prosciutto roughly into 16 portions and press

them into the dough. Sprinkle on the sage, mozzarella cheese and cracked black pepper. Mist the tops of the focaccias with a spray bottle and ladle water onto the empty baking sheet to create a burst of steam. Bake the focaccias until golden brown on top, about 15–20 minutes. Cool on racks before serving.

Il Barino Focaccia

I created this savoury and salty Italian flatbread while working in the kitchens of the former Il Barino Restaurant in Vancouver's trendy Yaletown. Make the dough as for Bambino Focaccia, but divide it into 4 portions. Top it with fresh minced garlic and herbs and a scattering of Parmesan cheese. Bake it as for Bambino Focaccia until it's golden brown on top. Drizzle with olive oil and sprinkle with coarse salt before serving.

Crispy Italian Potato Chip Sandwiches with Sage

These are truly addictive and definitely best served slightly warm with drinks before dinner.

Makes 3 dozen		Lesley Stowe
3 Tbsp.	olive oil	45 mL
3 Tbsp.	clarified butter	45 mL
3	russet (baking) potatoes, scrubbed	3
	fresh sage leaves	
1/2 cup	grated Parmesan cheese	120 mL

Combine the oil and butter. Lightly brush a parchment-lined baking sheet with the mixture. Using a mandoline, cut the potatoes one slice at a time 1/8–1/16 inch (.3–.15 cm) thick. Place a potato slice on the baking sheet and brush with the butter and oil mixture. Top with fresh sage. Cover with another potato slice, being careful to line up the edges. Brush with the butter and oil mixture. Continue until all the potatoes are sandwiched.

Bake at 300°F (150°C) until slightly golden and crispy, 10–15 minutes. You may need to turn them two-thirds of the way through the cooking. Remove the potatoes from the oven and sprinkle them with cheese. Return them to the oven briefly, for 30 seconds to 1 minute, to melt the cheese.

Chèvre Torte

Fresh local chèvre from the Okanagan or Salt Spring Island works beautifully for this. Serve sliced into wedges as an appetizer or for brunch. For a more elegant presentation and a shorter baking time, prepare individual ramekins.

Serves 6 generously or 8 as an appetizer		Glenys Morgan
1/2 cup	bread crumbs	120 mL
2–3 Tbsp.	finely ground walnuts or hazelnuts	30–45 mL
8 oz.	chèvre cheese	227 g
8 oz.	cream cheese	227 g
2	cloves garlic, finely minced	2
3	large eggs	3
1/2 tsp.	salt	2.5 mL
	freshly ground black pepper to taste	
2 Tbsp.	fresh tarragon, basil, chives, or a combination	30 mL

Preheat the oven to 350°F (175°C). Generously brush the inside of an 8-inch (20-cm) springform pan with softened butter. Combine the bread crumbs and nuts. (They may be ground together in the food processor.) Coat the inside of the pan with the crumb mixture. Rotate the pan to coat the sides and let any excess fall to the bottom. Shake the pan to level the crumbs.

Combine the cheeses, garlic, eggs, salt and pepper in a food processor. Blend, scraping down the sides of the bowl, until it's just smooth. Overprocessing causes cracks in the surface when baking. Add the fresh herbs to the workbowl. Pulse to chop and distribute them evenly in the batter.

Pour the batter into the prepared pan. Bake for 35–45 minutes. Check for a golden colour and shake the pan gently to see if the centre is firm. Cool 10–15 minutes before slicing or cool completely and serve at room temperature. It will fall naturally like a soufflé.

Gorgonzola & Pecan Soufflés

Many people think soufflés are hard to make, but this recipe proves they are quite simple. The most amazing thing is that they can be made the day before. At the restaurant we serve the soufflés on a small salad.

Serves 6		Tamara Kourchenko
1/3 cup	pecans, toasted and chopped fine	80 mL
4 1/2 Tbsp.	all-purpose flour	67.5 mL
3 Tbsp.	butter	45 mL
2/3 cup	whole milk	160 mL
3	egg yolks	3
6 oz.	Gorgonzola or Danish blue cheese, crumbled	170 g
	salt and black pepper to taste	
5	egg whites	5

Preheat the oven to 350°F (175°C). Mix the pecans with 1/2 Tbsp. (7.5 mL) flour. Butter six 1/2-cup (120-mL) ramekins and coat with the nut mixture. Set aside.

Melt the butter over low heat in a small saucepan. Add the remaining 4 Tbsp. (60 mL) flour and, stirring constantly, cook until it resembles wet sand and the mixture is light golden brown, about 5 minutes. Add the milk, stirring all the time, and cook until thick. Transfer to a bowl and whisk in the egg yolks and the cheese. Season with salt and pepper.

In a clean bowl of an electric mixer beat the egg whites until soft peaks form. Carefully, but thoroughly, adding 1/3 at a time, fold the egg whites into the cheese mixture. Divide the soufflé equally among the ramekins and place in an ovenproof pan. Fill the pan with hot water until it comes halfway up the sides of the ramekins. Bake for about 25 minutes.

The soufflés can be made one day ahead and reheated at 350°F (175°C) for about 10 minutes before serving.

Grilled & Stuffed Zucchini Rolls

These zucchini rolls are a fresh addition to your antipasto platter. If eggplant is a favourite, prepare half the recipe with zucchini and the other half with eggplant.

Makes about 20 rolls		Caren McSherry-Valagao
2	large firm zucchini	2
1/3 cup	sun-dried tomatoes	80 mL
1 cup	ricotta cheese	240 mL
1 tsp.	sea salt	5 mL
1 tsp.	freshly ground black pepper	5 mL
1 Tbsp.	chopped oregano or thyme	15 mL
3 Tbsp.	freshly snipped chives	45 mL
3 Tbsp.	chopped capers	45 mL
	fresh Parmesan shavings	

Trim the ends off the zucchini. Carefully slice them lengthwise into 1/8-inch (.3-cm) slices. If you have a mandoline, it works great.

Lightly brush the zucchini slices with olive oil. Grill or barbecue them for about 1 minute on each side, or until golden and soft enough to roll. Set aside. Pour boiling water over the sun-dried tomatoes; let them sit in the water for about 10 minutes. Drain, blot dry and coarsely chop. Mix together the cheese, salt, pepper, oregano or thyme, chives, capers and tomatoes. Stir well to combine all the ingredients.

Place the zucchini slices on your work surface and spoon about 1 Tbsp. (15 mL) of the filling onto one end of each slice. Roll the zucchini up and secure it with a toothpick if necessary. Lay the finished rolls on a colourful platter and garnish with shavings of Parmesan cheese.

Spicy Steamed Mussels with Tortilla Crumbs

What makes this mussel preparation unique is the crumbled tortillas that add texture and flavour to the sauce. Making this dish is actually an excuse for me to eat the sauce all by itself. I like to slurp it back with a spoon and share most of my mussels. Serve with bread, warm tortillas or corn chips. Chipotle chiles en adobo are available in large supermarkets and stores selling Latin American ingredients.

Serves 4 to 6		Karen Barnaby
3 lbs.	fresh mussels	1.4 kg
1 Tbsp.	olive oil	15 mL
1/2 tsp.	whole cumin seeds	2.5 mL
6	cloves garlic, minced	6
1/2 cup	finely diced onion	120 mL
1	28-oz. (796-mL) can plum tomatoes, well drained	1
1/2 cup	dry red wine	120 mL
2	canned chipotle chiles en adobo, finely chopped	2
1	large pinch allspice	1
2	fresh or frozen corn tortillas, crumbled into coarse crumbs	2
1/4 cup	coarsely chopped cilantro	60 mL
4	thin slices lime	4

Check over the mussels, removing any bits of "beard." Tap any mussels that are open and isolate them from the rest. If they do not close within a few minutes, discard them.

Heat the oil in a large, wide, heavy pot over medium-high heat. Add the cumin seeds. When they darken a shade, stir in the garlic and onion and cook until the onion browns lightly. Add the tomato, wine, chiles and allspice. Simmer over low heat for 10 minutes. The sauce may be prepared up to several hours in advance to this point.

Bring the sauce to a full boil and add the tortillas and mussels. Cover with a lid and steam until the mussels open, 5–10 minutes. Add the cilantro and lime and shake the pot to distribute the cilantro. Serve immediately in heated bowls.

Karen Barnaby

I hail from Ottawa where I started my cooking career in 1979 as a baker of carrot cakes and quiches on a pink, four-burner electric stove in the basement of the Bohemian Restaurant. Moving out of the basement and eventually out of Ottawa, I landed in Toronto in the winter of 1981, pounded the pavement of Queen Street, and met Steven, the love of my life—though not through pounding pavement. At that time, the owners of the Queen Mother Cafe were looking for a second chef to complement their new venture, called the Rivoli. After three years of listening to the new wave bands in the club at the back of the Rivoli (The Kids in the Hall, Jane Siberry and Blue Rodeo were fledgling acts there), and gratefully absorbing all the knowledge that chef Vanipha Southalack had to impart on Thai and Laotian cooking, I set my sights on the newly opened David Wood Food Shop in Rosedale. Through a fortuitous twist of fate in 1985, I found myself working there as a cook. After six months, David Wood promoted me to chef. It was a dream come true! During the five years there, I opened two more David Wood Food Shops and co-wrote the *David Wood Food Book* and the *David Wood Dessert Book*.

After five years at the David Wood Food Shop it was time to take a break and I spent the winter of 1990–91 in Cuernevaca, Mexico, as a private chef.

In the spring of 1991, Steven and I accepted job offers at the West Vancouver Capers location. After a year there, I was eager to engage in other Vancouver cooking adventures and was hired as chef of the Raintree Restaurant. In 1994, the Raintree became part of Concepts Restaurants, and as executive chef, I oversaw the opening of three restaurants: the Harvest Moon Cafe in Victoria, North 49 Restaurant and Market, and Restaurant Starfish and Oyster Bar. While at the Raintree, Whitecap Books invited me to write a book for them, and *Pacific Passions* was released in the fall of 1995. It has since sold 10,000 copies and has gone into a second printing.

In December of 1994, I was approached by Hubert Schmid of Kanke Seafood Restaurants to re-open the Fish House in Stanley Park as executive chef. I saw this as a perfect opportunity to share my cooking style and hone my management skills to the fullest.

My second book, *Screamingly Good Food*, was released in the fall of 1997. I am proud to say that it sold about 5,000 copies in three months.

While in Toronto, I discovered that I had an aptitude for teaching and put it into practice at Dufflet's Great Cooks Cooking School, a venue for Toronto's top chefs. I continue to teach at Tools and Techniques in West Vancouver, the Cook Shop in City Square and Caren's cooking school.

I don't think of myself as a ground-breaker, but as an interpreter, translator and teacher. I like a wide range of flavours and sensations, as screamingly hot and flavourful as Thai green curry or as soft and elusive as chestnut ice cream. A classic and properly made white clam linguine is my idea of heaven and so is a goat taco from a market stall in Mexico. I think budding chefs should study the origin and historical use of ingredients from other lands and learn how to use them traditionally before unleashing their ideas on the public. I feel embarrassed when I think of all the undercooked Thai black rice that was served in the late eighties.

My two grandmothers shaped my outlook on food. They were both on the fringe as far as cooking and eating in the sixties was concerned. They taught me how to eat avocados, artichokes, zucchini, eggplants and organ meats, how to pick wild garlic and strawberries and make marmalade out of mountain ash berries. They had no cultural or economic boundaries to hold them back from enjoying any kind of food, whether it was from the fields or the local IGA. Eating with them was always a discovery, and it is this experience that I crave.

My current projects include a collection of recipes by women chefs from across Canada who use their mothers' recipes, a book on old-fashioned desserts, and *More Screamingly Good Food*.

Steamed Mussels Marinera Style

Marinera style is typical of Spain, and it consists of cooking the shellfish with white wine, lots of garlic and parsley. Interestingly, they use bread crumbs to thicken the sauce. This is one of those wonderful dishes that take longer to describe than to make. Depending on the number of mussels you serve, this can be an appetizer or a light meal.

Serves 6		Tamara Kourchenko
6 Tbsp.	extra-virgin olive oil	90 mL
4	cloves garlic, finely chopped	4
48	mussels, washed and debearded	48
2 cups	white wine	475 mL
2 Tbsp.	fresh lemon juice	30 mL
1/2 cup	fresh bread crumbs	120 mL
3 Tbsp.	chopped parsley	45 mL
	salt and black pepper to taste	

Heat the oil in a pan or pot large enough to hold the mussels. Add the garlic, and as soon as it starts sizzling, add the mussels. Be careful not to burn the garlic, because this would give a bitter taste to the dish. Immediately add the wine, lemon juice, bread crumbs and parsley. Cover and cook until the mussels just open.

Remove the mussels to a shallow bowl. Season the sauce with salt and pepper and pour over the mussels. Use some good crusty bread to soak up the rest of the sauce.

Prawns with Pink Ginger & Lime Sauce

Gari, the sweet shaved ginger served with sushi, flatters prawns with its colour and flavour. A pastel pink colour means the ginger has been tinted. Natural gari is a honey colour with only a hint of pink. Larger grocery stores now sell it chilled in jars and vacuum packs, or visit your local Japanese restaurant to buy a small amount. For a little heat, add a seeded and slivered jalapeño pepper to the presentation.

Serves 4		Glenys Morgan
2 Tbsp.	finely minced shallots	30 mL
1	clove garlic, finely minced	1
4 Tbsp.	gari ginger with juice	60 mL
1	lime, zest and juice	1
2 Tbsp.	mirin (natural rice wine vinegar)	30 mL
6 Tbsp.	chilled unsalted butter, cut into 1/2-inch (1.2-cm) cubes	90 mL
1/4 tsp.	salt	1.2 mL
1 Tbsp.	oil or butter	15 mL
16–20	peeled prawns, depending on size	16–20
	cilantro leaves or chive sprigs	

In a non-reactive saucepan, combine the shallot and garlic. Drain the ginger, reserving 2 Tbsp. (30 mL) of the liquid. Finely mince the ginger and set aside. The drained liquid from the ginger combined with the lime juice and mirin should equal 1/2 cup (120 mL). Add this to the saucepan. Boil the mixture gently to reduce the liquid by 2/3. It will look like marmalade. This step may be completed ahead and finished later.

Over low heat, whisk in 2 pieces of butter. The sauce will look creamy white. Continue to whisk in the butter, piece by piece. Season with salt. Add the ginger and heat through gently.

Heat the 1 Tbsp. (15 mL) oil or butter in a skillet. Sear the prawns until just opaque and pink. Whisk the sauce. If it separates, add another pat of cold butter or if it's too thick, thin with a tablespoon (15 mL) of water. Serve the prawns with the sauce spooned lightly over and garnish with the lime zest and cilantro or chives.

Smoked Black Cod Brandade

Brandade is a traditional Provençal dish of salt cod that is served at the grand Christmas Eve dinner or as an appetizer during other times of the year. Salt cod requires advance planning as it has to be soaked a few days beforehand to soften and de-salt it. While using smoked black cod is not authentic, it certainly is delicious and fast. If you are familiar with the Greek taramasalata, you will immediately take a shine to brandade. Serve a plate of raw vegetables—fennel, cucumber, tomatoes, peppers and endive leaves—for dipping into the brandade along with toasted baguette.

Serves 6 to 8		Karen Barnaby
3/4 lb.	russet potatoes (2 medium)	340 g
4 cups	water	950 mL
1	bay leaf	1
1 Tbsp.	salt	15 mL
10	black peppercorns	10
1	whole dried chile	1
1 lb.	naturally smoked black cod fillet, cut into 4 pieces	454 g
1/4 cup	fruity extra-virgin olive oil, warmed	60 mL
1/4 cup	milk, warmed	60 mL
2	cloves garlic, minced and mashed to a paste with 1/4 tsp. (1.2 mL) salt	2
1 Tbsp.	lemon juice	15 mL
	salt and freshly ground black pepper to taste	
	black olives	

Cook the potatoes in their skins in abundant boiling water until tender, 30–40 minutes. Drain and cool until easy to handle, but still warm. Peel the potatoes, cut them into chunks and mash by hand until smooth.

While the potatoes are cooking, combine the water, bay leaf, salt, peppercorns, and chile in a medium pot. Bring to a boil and add the cod. Cover and turn the heat down to low. Simmer for 10–12 minutes until just cooked through. Remove to a plate with a slotted spoon. Remove the skin and bones from the cod and flake the fish. Add it to the potatoes. With an electric mixer or a whisk, beat the cod and potatoes until they start to "mass" together. Slowly beat in the olive oil, milk, garlic paste and lemon juice. Mix until smooth and creamy. Season with salt and pepper (it should be a bit on the salty side).

Serve the brandade warm or at room temperature; do not refrigerate. Spread it out on a large plate and drizzle with a fruity, extra-virgin olive oil. Garnish with the olives and serve with toasted baguette and vegetables as above, if you wish.

Tomato Prawn Bruschetta

We have all made or at least eaten the traditional bruschetta with tomatoes and garlic but this is hardly any more work and the results are sublime. Try serving these with a salad of mixed greens for a luncheon or starter course.

Makes 3 dozen		Lesley Stowe
1 lb.	prawns, shelled	454 g
1	lemon, zest only, cut in julienne strips	1
1 tsp.	lemon juice	5 mL
2 Tbsp.	capers	30 mL
3 Tbsp.	minced fresh basil	45 mL
4	cloves garlic, minced	4
4 Tbsp.	olive oil	60 mL
1 1/2 cups	tomatoes, seeded and diced (approximately 7 Romas)	360 mL
	salt and black pepper to taste	
1	baguette or ficelle, sliced 1/2 inch (1.2 cm) thick and grilled	1

Blanch the prawns in 10 cups (2.4 L) of water until they are just cooked, approximately 2–4 minutes. Place in a bowl of ice-cold water to stop the cooking. Drain. When they are cool, chop the prawns into 1/4-inch (.6-cm) pieces.

Mix together the lemon zest, lemon juice, capers, basil, garlic, olive oil and tomatoes. Season with salt and pepper. Mix in the prawns. Spoon 1–2 Tbsp. (15–30 mL) of the topping on each slice of grilled baguette. Serve immediately.

Prawn-tinis

A prawn cocktail served in a martini glass. Despite my culinary training, I still like to serve this with store-bought cocktail sauce (just go to a good store!). I figure, if it ain't broke, why fix it?

Serves 4		Mary Mackay
20	tiger prawns	20
1	stalk lemon grass	1
4 1/4 cups	water	1 L
5	whole peppercorns, crushed	5
5	cloves garlic, smashed	5
1 tsp.	salt	5 mL
8	green olives, stuffed with pimento	8
1/4 cup	cocktail sauce	60 mL
2 Tbsp.	prepared mayonnaise	30 mL
2 cups	mixed baby lettuce	475 mL
1/2	lemon, cut into 4 wedges	1/2

Remove the shells from the tiger prawns, leaving the tails intact. Place the shells in a medium saucepan. De-vein the prawns and set aside. Cut 6 inches (15 cm) off the top of the lemon grass stalk and set aside. Chop the remaining lemon grass into 1/2-inch (1.2-cm) pieces. Add the lemon grass, water, peppercorns, garlic cloves and salt to the pan with the prawn shells and bring to a boil over medium-high heat. Let cool to room temperature. Strain the stock through a fine sieve. Return the liquid to the pot and bring to a boil. Stir in the prawns and remove from the heat. Let the prawns poach for about 30 seconds, until pink. Remove the prawns from the stock and cool to room temperature.

Make a hole in each olive with a toothpick or bamboo skewer. Separate the reserved stalk of lemon grass into 4 skewers and slide 2 green olives onto each. In a small bowl, stir together the cocktail sauce and mayonnaise.

To assemble, line the martini glasses with the mixed baby lettuce and top with a dollop of cocktail mayonnaise. Place 5 prawns, evenly spaced, head first into the cocktail mayonnaise, leaving their tails hanging over the edge of the glass. Place a lemon grass skewer of olives in the middle of the glass, leaning to one side, and garnish with a lemon wedge. Cheers!

Smoked Salmon Pinwheel

An easy appetizer that can be made in minutes. If goat cheese is not your favourite, use cream cheese for a simple alternative. Roasted vegetables can be substituted for the salmon, for a vegetarian version. I often use the coloured flour tortillas that are readily available in supermarkets.

Makes 30 pieces		Caren McSherry-Valagao
2 Tbsp.	olive oil	30 mL
3	large shallots, thinly sliced	3
1 lb.	goat cheese	454 g
1 Tbsp.	horseradish	15 mL
10	flour tortillas, 8-inch (20-cm) size	10
	freshly cracked pepper to taste	
1 lb.	sliced smoked salmon	454 g
1	bunch fresh dill	1

Heat the olive oil in a small pan. Add the shallots and fry until crispy. Drain on paper towel. Combine the goat cheese with the horseradish and shallots.

Lay the tortillas flat on your work surface and spread the cheese mixture evenly over them. Generously grind pepper over the cheese. Place the smoked salmon on top of the cheese in a single, even layer. Place some dill in the centre of each tortilla, forming a line down the centre.

Firmly roll the tortilla up, jelly-roll fashion. Make sure it is tight so it will not come apart when slicing. Wrap each roll tightly in plastic wrap and chill until serving time.

To serve, slice on the diagonal into 1/2-inch (1.2-cm) slices.

Chilean Sea Bass with Arugula, Crispy Potatoes & Tapenade

Sea bass has become very popular and deservedly so. It is moist, silky in texture and full-flavoured. I pair it here with tapenade, the black olive paste from Provence. This appetizer with a glass of crisp white wine heightens the appetite for the next course.

Serves 4		Margaret Chisholm
3 Tbsp.	extra-virgin olive oil	45 mL
2 Tbsp.	orange juice	30 mL
1 tsp.	white wine vinegar	5 mL
10 oz.	boneless skinless sea bass	285 g
	salt and freshly ground black pepper to taste	
1	russet or Yukon Gold potato, peeled	1
1 Tbsp.	melted butter	15 mL
	salt to taste	
1	small handful arugula or mixed wild greens	1
3 Tbsp.	Tapenade	45 mL

Preheat the oven to 400°F (200°C). Whisk together the oil, orange juice and vinegar in a small bowl and set aside. Cut the fish into 4 slices, each 1/2 inch thick (1.2 cm). Sprinkle with salt and pepper and place on a non-stick pan.

Slice the potato very thinly, approximately 1/8 inch (.3 cm). A mandoline or other slicing tool will make this easier. Place on a non-stick baking sheet and brush with melted butter. Sprinkle with salt. Bake for approximately 10 minutes or until golden brown. Halfway through the cooking, place the sea bass in the oven.

Arrange the arugula in the centre of 4 plates. Top with 3 slices of potato. When the fish is just barely firm to the touch, remove it from the oven and spread each piece with 2 tsp. (10 mL) of the tapenade. Place the fish on top of the potatoes. Drizzle the fish and the surrounding plate with the olive oil mixture. Serve at once.

Tapenade

Makes 1/2 cup (120 mL)

Tapenade will keep in the refrigerator for a week or so. Put it in a small ramekin, smooth the surface and cover with a thin film of olive oil. It is delicious on hard-boiled eggs, new potatoes or crostini.

1	clove garlic, coarsely chopped	1
4	anchovies	4
2 Tbsp.	capers	30 mL
1/3 cup	pitted black olives, niçoise or sun-dried	80 mL
2 tsp.	Dijon mustard	10 mL
2 Tbsp.	extra-virgin olive oil	30 mL
	freshly ground black pepper to taste	
1/4 tsp.	fresh thyme leaves	1.2 mL

Place all the ingredients in a food processor and process to a rough textured paste, about 15 seconds. You can also make the tapenade by putting all the ingredients on a board and chopping and mashing to a paste.

Pizza with Arugula Pesto, Caramelized Onion & Provolone

The dough recipe will make 6 small or 3 medium pizzas, but I pop extra dough in the freezer. I prefer to go easy on the amount of topping so that all the flavours and textures are discernible.

Makes 4 small pizzas		Deb Connors

For the pizza dough:

1 Tbsp.	dry yeast	15 mL
2 tsp.	honey	10 mL
1 cup	warm water	240 mL
3 cups	unbleached flour	720 mL
1 1/2 tsp.	salt	7.5 mL
1 1/2 tsp.	olive oil	7.5 mL

In a small bowl dissolve the yeast and honey in 1/4 cup (60 mL) of the warm water. Let sit until the mixture starts to bubble, 5–8 minutes.

In a mixing bowl with a dough hook, combine the flour and salt. With the mixer on medium-low, add the olive oil and yeast mixture. Add the remaining 3/4 cup (180 mL) warm water and knead for 5 minutes, until the dough becomes smooth and elastic. Remove the dough, place it in a greased bowl, cover it with a damp towel and allow it to rest in a warm place for 30 minutes.

Flatten the dough and divide it into 6 equal pieces. Stretch and work each piece of dough and roll it tightly into a ball. (The 2 extra pieces of dough can be plastic-wrapped and frozen at this point.) Cover the dough again with a damp towel and let rest for 20 more minutes.

Place the balls of dough on a lightly floured surface and roll each into an 8-inch (20-cm) circle, 1/4 inch (.6 cm) thick. If you are making the pizza dough ahead, you can stack the individual pieces of rolled dough with waxed paper between each one. Cover snugly with plastic wrap and refrigerate.

For the arugula pesto:

3/4 cup	arugula leaves, packed	180 mL
1/2 cup	basil leaves, packed	120 mL
2	cloves garlic	2
1 tsp.	lemon juice	5 mL

1/2 cup	grated Parmesan cheese	120 mL
1/2 tsp.	salt	2.5 mL
1/2 tsp.	freshly ground black pepper	2.5 mL
1/4 cup	olive oil	60 mL

In a food processor fitted with a blade, combine the arugula, basil, garlic, lemon juice, cheese, salt and pepper. With the motor running, slowly add the olive oil until the pesto is finely chopped and well blended. This may be made a day ahead, covered and refrigerated. Bring to room temperature 1 hour before using.

For the caramelized onion:

3 Tbsp.	olive oil	45 mL
3	medium white onions, cut in half, sliced 1/4 inch (.6 cm) thick	3
1/4 cup	balsamic vinegar	60 mL

Heat the olive oil in a large, heavy-bottomed sauté pan over medium-high heat. Add the onions and cook, stirring frequently, until nicely browned, about 10 minutes. Reduce the heat to medium-low, add the balsamic vinegar and continue cooking until the onions are soft, approximately 10 minutes. Set aside to cool.

For the potato:

8	small potatoes	8
	salt to taste	

Boil the potatoes in salted water until just tender. Cool and cut in 1/4-inch (.6-cm) slices.

To assemble:

4	pizza shells	4
3/4 cup	arugula pesto	180 mL
	caramelized onions	
8	boiled, sliced potatoes	8
	salt and freshly ground black pepper to taste	
16	slices provolone, 1/4 inch (.6 cm) thick	16

Preheat the oven to 500ºF (260ºC). Cover each pizza with arugula pesto, spreading it as thinly as possible, leaving a 1/2-inch (1.2-cm) border on the edge of the pizza. Evenly distribute the caramelized onion. Top with slices of potato. Season with salt and pepper. Top each pizza with 4 slices of provolone cheese, slightly overlapped. Bake in the oven until the edges of the pizza are golden brown, and the cheese is nicely melted. Remove from the oven and lightly brush the edges of each pizza with olive oil.

Slow-Braised Quail with Eight Favourite Flavours

Using this slow and gentle cooking procedure infuses the quail with the flavours of the other ingredients. The meat turns meltingly tender and can be spread on a slice of good baguette, almost like a pâté. You can serve the quails au naturel with a great pile of bread to absorb the juices or on the Salad of Bitter Greens with Walnut Oil Dressing (page 32). It is of the greatest importance that the casserole be completely sealed by the flour paste. This is one of those dishes that make me scream.

Serves 4		Karen Barnaby
4	large quails	4
4 oz.	prosciutto, in one piece	113 g
8	cloves garlic, peeled	8
1/2 tsp.	salt	2.5 mL
2 oz.	good-quality green olives	57 g
2 oz.	good-quality black olives	57 g
1/4 tsp.	black peppercorns	1.2 mL
1/4 tsp.	coriander seeds	1.2 mL
4	strips lemon peel, yellow part only	4
4	2-inch (5-cm) sprigs fresh rosemary	4
2 Tbsp.	dry white wine	30 mL
2 Tbsp.	fruity extra-virgin olive oil	30 mL
1 cup	flour	240 mL

Preheat the oven to 250°F (120°C). Choose a small baking dish or pot with a tight-fitting lid that will hold the quails snugly in a single layer.

Wash the quails and pat them dry. Cut the prosciutto into 2- x 1/4-inch (5- x .6-cm) strips. Place 2 strips of prosciutto and 1 clove of garlic in the cavity of each quail. Sprinkle all sides of the quails with the salt.

Spread 1/2 the remaining prosciutto, and the olives, peppercorns and coriander seeds on the bottom of the baking dish. Arrange the quails on top. Spread the remaining prosciutto over the quails. Tuck the lemon peel, rosemary and remaining garlic in between the quails. Pour the white wine and olive oil over the quails and cover with the lid. Combine the flour with enough water to form a thick, moldable paste. Form into thick ropes and press in a continuous line around the lid to seal the casserole tightly. Place on the middle shelf of the oven and bake for 4 hours.

Remove the casserole from the oven and gently tap the hardened flour paste around the casserole with a knife to break the seal and carefully remove the lid. Do this at the table so everyone can enjoy the fantastic aroma that will be unleashed.

Salads

Salad of Bitter Greens with Walnut Oil Dressing

This is a great salad—sitting prettily under the Slow Braised Quail with Eight Favourite Flavours (page 28) or on its own with an inspired sprinkling of blue cheese and toasted walnuts. It has taken me 20 years to realize that if you don't use the chicory stems and the thick white base of radicchio leaves they will make a better salad—taste-wise and texturally.

Serves 4		Karen Barnaby
1	medium head chicory, washed and dried	1
1/4	head radicchio	1/4
1 Tbsp.	finely chopped shallots	15 mL
1/4 tsp.	salt	1.2 mL
1 tsp.	Dijon mustard	5 mL
2 tsp.	balsamic vinegar	10 mL
1 tsp.	red wine vinegar	5 mL
1 tsp.	lemon juice	5 mL
3 Tbsp.	extra-virgin olive oil	45 mL
2 Tbsp.	good-quality walnut oil	30 mL

Pluck the curly, toothed "leaves" from each stem of chicory and place in a bowl. Discard the stems or save them for soup. Tear the radicchio into 1-inch (2.5-cm) pieces, discarding the thick, white base of the leaves. Cover with a damp towel and place in the refrigerator.

Combine the shallots, salt, mustard, vinegars and lemon juice in a small bowl. Mix well with a fork. Slowly beat in the oils. Refrigerate until ready to serve. Toss the salad with the dressing just before serving.

Baby Spinach Salad with French Roquefort

This is not only a beautiful salad, but also a lot of fun to eat, because of the contrast of flavours and textures. I usually prepare it for New Year's Dinner because pomegranate seeds represent life and fertility in some cultures, and those are good things to start the year with. Pomegranates are only available from late September to the beginning of January.

Serves 6		Tamara Kourchenko
3 oz.	hazelnuts	85 g
1	pomegranate	1
8 oz.	baby spinach	225 g
4 oz.	French Roquefort, crumbled	113 g
1/2 cup	Balsamic Vinaigrette	120 mL

Preheat the oven to 350°F (175°C). Spread the hazelnuts on a cookie sheet and bake for about 15 minutes or until golden brown. Cool and coarsely chop. Cut the pomegranate in half and carefully take out the seeds. Discard the white pith. Combine the spinach, half the hazelnuts, the crumbled Roquefort and half the pomegranate seeds in a large bowl. Toss with the vinaigrette. Divide among 6 plates and garnish with the remaining hazelnuts and pomegranate seeds.

Balsamic Vinaigrette

Makes 2 cups (475 mL)

This vinaigrette will keep, covered, in the refrigerator for 2 weeks.

1	shallot, finely chopped	1
2 tsp.	Dijon mustard	10 mL
1/2 cup	balsamic vinegar	120 mL
3/4 cup	extra-virgin olive oil	180 mL
3/4 cup	vegetable oil	180 mL
	salt and black pepper to taste	

Combine the shallot, Dijon mustard and balsamic vinegar in a bowl. Slowly whisk in both oils in a steady stream. Season with salt and pepper.

Tamara Kourchenko

I was born and raised in Mexico City. I've been baking ever since I was a little girl: Christmas cookies with my German grandmother and doughnuts and cakes with my mother. Cooking and eating were always ways to celebrate, to thank, to give. We used to bake a cake at home for every birthday in my family, and the older we got, the more elaborate and difficult they were. Every special occasion was marked by a big meal.

After finishing high school, like most teenagers, I had no idea what I wanted to do with myself. Since I always loved cooking I decided to work in a restaurant to see if I liked it, so I got a six-month apprenticeship in a fine dining Spanish restaurant called Babieca.

Since I couldn't find a cooking school I liked in Mexico City, I decided to go to university and graduated with a degree in Hotel and Restaurant Management from the Universidad Iberoamericana. Again, the courses I enjoyed the most were the ones related to cooking. That's why, in 1990, I decided to go to the Culinary Institute of America in Hyde Park, New York. It was there I met Philip, my love, my partner, my friend.

Two years after, when we graduated, we moved to Boston, Massachusetts. There I worked for Jody Adams in a restaurant in Cambridge called Michela's. I started there as a café cook and moved up to be the sous-chef. The two years I spent with Jody marked my style and the way I think about food. She is one of the most important influences in my career.

Once our visas expired, Philip and I had to move again. This time we had to choose between Canada and Mexico, but since Philip doesn't speak Spanish we moved to Vancouver, close to his family. Here, the first one to give me a job was Adam Busby at Star Anise. Then I was very lucky to meet Karen Barnaby and Steve McKinley. I worked with them at Restaurant Starfish and Oyster Bar and North 49 Restaurant and Market.

It was during that time, 1995, that Phil and I found the location for our restaurant. It was a 1912 brick building with an inner courtyard. We fell in love with it and, on July 9, 1995, we opened Farrago Restaurant at 1138 Homer Street. We called it Farrago, because it means mixture, and that is exactly what we are: I come from Mexico, Phil comes from B.C, we met in New York, and we cook French, Italian and Spanish food.

In March 1997 we made some changes to the restaurant, dividing it in two and opening a bistro area with more casual food. Now it's called Farrago Restaurant and Bistro.

I really enjoy having a restaurant with my husband. It's like entertaining each night of the week. I love going to the market and choosing vegetables and trying different kinds of meat and fish. To me, the perfect dish has to have a combination and contrast of flavours, colours and textures.

There is nothing more satisfying than to see people enjoying your food and having a good time. I believe that eating should be fun, that every meal should be unique in a way. It doesn't matter if it consists of a messy hot dog in a baseball stadium or a romantic rack of lamb dinner at home. I guess that is why I love cooking: I like to make people happy.

Crispy Asiago Cups with Tomato Salad

These crisp bowls of cheese are like the best part of a grilled cheese sandwich—the crispy, chewy bits at the edges. They are delicious on their own with a glass of chilled white wine or filled with ripe tomatoes and lettuce. If you have never used sherry vinegar, try it as an alternative to the more popular balsamic for a nice change.

Serves 4		Margaret Chisholm
1 tsp.	unsalted butter	5 mL
1/4 lb.	Asiago cheese, grated	113 g
1	head butter lettuce	1
2	ripe tomatoes	2
	salt and freshly ground black pepper to taste	
1 recipe	Sherry Shallot Vinaigrette	1 recipe

Melt 1/4 of the 1 tsp. (5 mL) of butter in a small non-stick pan over medium-low heat. When the butter foams, spread 1/4 of the cheese in a thin layer in the pan. Cook until the cheese begins to firm up. Pour off the oil into a small bowl. Continue to cook until the cheese is a very pale golden brown.

Lift carefully out of the pan and shape over the bottom of a tea cup or ramekin. Repeat until you have prepared 4 cheese cups. Set aside to cool.

Trim, wash and tear the lettuce into pieces. Cut the tomatoes into 3/4-inch (2-cm) chunks and toss with a little salt and pepper. Toss the lettuce and tomatoes with the vinaigrette. Fill the Asiago cups with the lettuce and tomato mixture and serve immediately.

Sherry Shallot Vinaigrette

Makes 1/3 cup (80 mL)

1 Tbsp.	sherry vinegar	15 mL
2 tsp.	Dijon mustard	10 mL
1/8 tsp.	salt	.5 mL
1/4 cup	extra-virgin olive oil	60 mL
1 1/2 Tbsp.	shallots, very finely chopped	22.5 mL
1 Tbsp.	chopped chives	15 mL
	freshly ground black pepper to taste	

Whisk the vinegar, mustard and salt together in a medium bowl. Slowly add the oil a few drops at a time while whisking. Continue to whisk while pouring the oil in a steady stream. Stir in the shallots and chives. Season generously with pepper.

Warm Shredded Bread Salad

A salad of bread, torn into shreds, toasted and tossed with balsamic vinaigrette, tomatoes, bocconcini and basil.

Serves 4		Mary Mackay
1 tsp.	Dijon mustard	5 mL
1 tsp.	honey	5 mL
1/2 tsp.	salt	2.5 mL
1/4 cup	balsamic vinegar	60 mL
1/2 cup	olive oil	120 mL
1/2	loaf sourdough bread, day old, crust removed	1/2
7 oz.	feta cheese, crumbled	200 g
4	Roma tomatoes, cut into 6 wedges each	4
12	fresh basil leaves, shredded	12
	cracked black pepper to taste	

In a bowl whisk together the mustard, honey, salt and vinegar. Continue whisking while slowly adding the oil. Set the vinaigrette aside.

Preheat the oven to 400°F (200°C). Shred the bread into bite-size pieces (about 40 pieces). Place on a baking sheet and toast for about 7 minutes. Remove and toss with the vinaigrette, feta cheese, tomato wedges and shredded basil. Divide among 4 plates and garnish with cracked black pepper.

Fresh Herb Salad with Grilled Mushrooms & Tomatoes

Herbs play a reversed role in this salad—not quietly snipped into the dressing but boldly making the greens come alive. In summer, it helps me keep my basil, arugula and parsley trimmed. From the market in winter, I buy smaller bunches and make a wonderful salad for four. Excellent with sliced grilled steak or, for a meatless meal, grilled polenta wedges.

Serves 4 to 6		Glenys Morgan
1 cup	basil leaves, loosely packed	240 mL
1 cup	Italian parsley leaves, coarse stems trimmed	240 mL
1	bunch arugula or watercress, or a combination, trimmed and washed	1
1/3 cup	balsamic vinegar	80 mL
1/3 cup	extra-virgin olive oil	80 mL
2–3	portobello mushrooms, stems removed	2–3
	salt and freshly ground black pepper to taste	
3–4	vine-ripened tomatoes, quartered or sliced	3–4

Reserve 1/4 cup (60 mL) each of the basil and parsley, then mix the remaining leaves with the arugula or watercress. Chill the greens until 1/2 hour before using, but do not serve them cold. Place on a platter or individual plates.

Finely chop the reserved basil and parsley, or whiz in a blender with the vinegar and oil until combined.

Heat the barbecue, stove-top grill or a heavy pan for searing the mushrooms. For stove grilling, the mushrooms should be cut into 1-inch (2.5-cm) strips. On a larger grill, they may be cooked whole and sliced after. Brush the grill, not the mushrooms, with oil. When the grill is very hot, sear the mushrooms. They should brown and sear like steak. Season with salt and pepper when cooked. Remove from the grill and toss with 2/3 of the dressing.

Place the mushrooms on the base layer of greens. Layer the tomatoes on the mushrooms and drizzle with the last of the dressing. Each layer should be slightly smaller to show all the colours. This salad is delicious served when the mushrooms are warm; as it cools the flavours blend nicely.

Billy Goat's Greens

I really like the contrast of food textures offered by this dish: crunchy toasted pumpkin seeds matched with soft warm goat cheese and crisp greens. It can be served as a wonderful light luncheon all by itself, or as a great start to a major dinner party.

Serves 4		Mary Mackay
1 tsp.	shallots, finely chopped	5 mL
1/8 tsp.	salt	.5 mL
2 tsp.	liquid honey	10 mL
1/3 cup	cranberry juice	80 mL
1/4 cup	vegetable oil	60 mL
2 Tbsp.	sun-dried cranberries	30 mL
1/2 cup	pumpkin seeds	120 mL
7 oz.	goat cheese	200 g
6 cups	mixed baby lettuce	1.5 L

Whisk together the shallots, salt, honey and cranberry juice. Slowly pour in the vegetable oil while continuing to whisk. Stir in the sun-dried cranberries and set the cranberry vinaigrette aside.

Preheat the oven to 400°F (200°C). Roast the pumpkin seeds in a shallow pan for 5–7 minutes. Cool and chop coarsely. Divide the goat cheese into 4 equal portions and shape each into a thick disk, 2 1/2 × 1/2 inch (6.2 × 1.2 cm). Roll each disk in pumpkin seeds to coat it completely. Place the coated disks in the refrigerator until ready to serve.

To assemble the salad, broil the goat cheese disks for 1 1/2 minutes on each side in a shallow pan. Toss the mixed baby lettuce with the cranberry vinaigrette, and divide among 4 plates. Top each salad with a warm goat cheese disk.

Grilled Caesar Salad with Parmesan Crisps & Reggiano Shavings

How can you fail to have a great dinner party when you include a Caesar Salad? This one is sure to impress your guests. Use large dinner plates to accommodate the full leaves of romaine, and good Parmesan is an absolute must. Ficelle is a skinny baguette with a dense crumb.

Serves 8		Lesley Stowe
3/4 cup	olive oil	180 mL
6	cloves garlic, chopped in half lengthwise	6
4	tight hearts of romaine (core attached)	4
	salt and black pepper to taste	
1	ficelle or baguette, day old	1
2 cups	grated Parmesan cheese	475 mL
1 recipe	Caesar Dressing	1 recipe
	Reggiano shavings	

Combine the oil and garlic in a small pan. Slowly bring to a boil. Remove from the heat and let rest for 30 minutes. Reserve half for the Parmesan crisps.

Rinse and dry the romaine. Slice each heart into quarters lengthwise and brush with the garlic oil. Season with salt and pepper. Set aside for grilling.

To make the Parmesan crisps, use ficelle that is at least a day old; otherwise it is too difficult to cut into even slices. Cut the ficelle on a 45-degree angle into 1/16-inch (.15-cm) slices. Line a baking sheet with parchment paper and lay the bread slices in a single layer on the baking sheet. Brush the top side of each slice with garlic oil and sprinkle with cheese. Bake at 250°F (120°C) for 15–20 minutes. They should be crisp and slightly golden.

Preheat the grill to high. Grill the romaine approximately 5–10 seconds on each side. For each serving, place 2 quarters of the grilled romaine on a large plate. Lean 2 Parmesan crisps against the romaine. Spoon 3–4 Tbsp. (45–60 mL) of Caesar Dressing over the romaine. Garnish with Reggiano shavings and serve immediately.

Caesar Dressing

Makes 2 cups (475 mL)

1/2 tsp.	hot pepper sauce	2.5 mL
1 tsp.	Worcestershire sauce	5 mL
1 Tbsp.	white wine vinegar	15 mL
1 Tbsp.	red wine vinegar	15 mL
2 Tbsp.	balsamic vinegar	30 mL
1 tsp.	Dijon mustard	5 mL
1	egg	1
3	cloves garlic	3
2–3	anchovies	2–3
1/2	lemon, juice only	1/2
1 1/2 cups	olive oil	360 mL
	salt to taste	
1 tsp.	black pepper	5 mL

Combine all the ingredients except the olive oil, salt and pepper. Mix by hand or in a food processor until well mixed. Slowly add the olive oil until emulsified. Season to taste with salt and pepper.

Roasted Two-Tomato Salad

I created this salad when the beautiful hot-house tomatoes came to market. This is a good way to break away from the traditional way of serving tomato salads, whether you grow your own or purchase them.

Serves 0 to 8		Caren McSherry-Valagao
8	good-quality red tomatoes	8
8	good-quality yellow tomatoes	8
4	purple onions, peeled	4
24	cloves garlic, peeled	24
4 tsp.	sugar	20 mL
1 tsp.	sea salt	5 mL
1–2 tsp.	freshly cracked black pepper	5–10 mL
1/3 cup	extra-virgin olive oil	80 mL
3 Tbsp.	balsamic vinegar	45 mL
4 Tbsp.	extra-virgin olive oil for drizzling	60 mL
	fresh arugula	

Preheat the oven to 400°F (200°C).

Slice the tomatoes into thirds lengthwise, approximately 1/3-inch (.8-cm) slices. Place the tomatoes on a stainless steel baking sheet. (If you don't have stainless, line what you have with foil.) Cut the onion into 6 wedges. Place the onion wedges and garlic cloves along the edges of the pan. Sprinkle the sugar evenly over the tomatoes. Season evenly with the sea salt and pepper. Drizzle with the 1/3 cup (80 mL) olive oil. Bake uncovered for about 25 minutes, or until the tomatoes are soft and beginning to brown.

Remove the tomatoes from the pan and set aside. Continue to cook the onions and garlic for an additional 20 minutes, or until they are soft and golden brown.

To serve, place 3 slices of red tomato and 3 slices of yellow tomato on each salad plate. Surround the tomatoes with some of the onion wedges and garlic cloves. Drizzle with the balsamic vinegar and olive oil. Season with additional sea salt and pepper if necessary. Garnish with fresh arugula if available.

Tomato Avocado Salad with Crispy Pancetta

I first had a version of this salad at a wonderful little food shop in Toronto. It is definitely a summer salad—when tomatoes are at their best and peppers are cheap and plentiful. Eat it the day it is made, as it will get soggy if left for more than a few hours.

Serves 8 to 10		Lesley Stowe
7 oz.	pancetta	200 g
1 lb.	red bell peppers	454 g
1 lb.	yellow bell peppers	454 g
3 1/2 lbs.	ripe tomatoes	1.6 kg
3 oz.	shallots	85 g
4	ripe avocados	4
3/4 cup	olive oil	180 mL
1/4 cup	cider vinegar	60 mL
8	large basil leaves	8
	salt and black pepper to taste	

Preheat the oven to 400°F (200°C). Slice the pancetta into thin slices, 1/16 inch (.15 cm). Place them on a baking sheet and bake for 10–15 minutes, or until crispy. Drain on paper towel. Chop coarsely into 1/2-inch (1.2-cm) pieces.

Cut the red and yellow peppers into 1-inch (2.5-cm) triangles. Cut the tomatoes into quarters, then into chunks. Cut the shallots in half and slice them across the grain. Dice the avocado into large chunks, 1 1/4 inches (3 cm).

Whisk the olive oil into the cider vinegar. Cut the basil leaves into fine strips. Gently toss the vinaigrette with the vegetables, basil and pancetta. Season with salt and pepper. Serve immediately.

Frisée with Hand-Peeled Shrimp, Fennel & Apple Cilantro Vinaigrette

This is another salad that can be used as a main course. Buy the freshest, best-quality shrimp. The vinaigrette adds texture and bright flavours; the fennel, a wonderful crunch.

Serves 4		Deb Connors
1	bulb fennel	1
2	small heads curly endive	2
8 oz.	fresh hand-peeled shrimp	225 g
1 recipe	Apple Cilantro Vinaigrette	1 recipe

Cut the fennel bulb in half lengthwise, remove the core and slice crosswise as thinly as possible. Submerge it in ice water for 1–1 1/2 hours before serving. This will crisp and curl the fennel.

Pull the curly endive apart, discarding the outer leaves and stem. Soak the leaves in cold water and pat dry.

Arrange the curly endive in the centres of 4 salad plates. Arrange 2 oz. (57 g) of shrimp on each plate on top of and among the leaves. Drizzle the vinaigrette over the salad and onto the plate. Spoon some of the apples and peppers out of the vinaigrette and place in 1 or 2 small stacks on each plate. Place a small stack of shaved fennel atop each salad.

Apple Cilantro Vinaigrette

Makes about 1 1/4 cups (300 mL)

1/4	red bell pepper, seeds and membrane removed, finely diced	1/4
1/4	yellow bell pepper, seeds and membrane removed, finely diced	1/4
1 Tbsp.	finely diced red onion	15 mL
1/2	Granny Smith apple, peeled and cored, finely diced	1/2
2 Tbsp.	fresh lemon juice	30 mL
1/2 cup	rice vinegar	120 mL
1 Tbsp.	chopped cilantro	15 mL
1/2 tsp.	salt	2.5 mL
1/2 tsp.	freshly ground black pepper	2.5 mL
1/2 cup	olive oil	120 mL

In a small bowl combine the diced peppers, onion and apple. Stir in the lemon juice. In a separate small bowl whisk together the rice vinegar, cilantro and salt and pepper. Slowly whisk in the olive oil. Combine with the other ingredients. Make this vinaigrette at least 1 hour before serving. Serve at room temperature.

Wild Rice & Papaya Salad

I developed this recipe for catering. It works equally well for a picnic for 4 or as a gala buffet for 4,000. Feel free to play with the ingredients, using other fresh or dried fruit; just make sure it is moist and seasoned well with salt and pepper.

Serves 4 to 6		Margaret Chisholm
1/2 cup	wild rice	120 mL
3/4 cup	white rice	180 mL
1 1/2 cups	water	360 mL
1/4 cup	orange juice	60 mL
2 tsp.	white wine vinegar	10 mL
1/4 cup	extra-virgin olive oil	60 mL
1/4 cup	dried apricots, diced	60 mL
1	small papaya, diced	1
1	red bell pepper, diced	1
1/4 cup	chopped cilantro	60 mL
1	green onion, sliced	1
	salt and freshly ground black pepper	

Rinse the wild rice in a colander and place in a small pot. Add enough water to cover by 2 inches (5 cm). Add a pinch of salt. Bring to a simmer and cook gently for approximately 45 minutes or until tender. Drain and set aside.

Meanwhile, place the white rice in a small pot with a tight-fitting lid. Add the water and a pinch of salt. Bring to a boil and simmer for approximately 20 minutes, or until the water is absorbed and the rice is tender. Place the rice in a serving bowl and set aside to cool.

Whisk together the orange juice, vinegar and olive oil. Combine the wild and white rice with the olive oil mixture, apricots, papaya, red pepper, cilantro and green onion. Season with salt and pepper.

Ahi Tuna Niçoise

The key to any wonderful fish dish is wonderful fish. The tuna must be very fresh. The tuna steaks should be 1 1/2–2 inches (3.8–5 cm) thick: this will allow you to quickly sear it on the outside while leaving the inside rare to medium-rare. Tuna is tough and dry if cooked past medium-rare. I like to serve this salad as a main course.

Serves 4		Deb Connors
8 cups	mesclun greens, loosely packed	2 L
4	small cooked potatoes, cut into 1/2-inch (1.2-cm) dice	4
4 oz.	green beans, blanched and slivered	113 g
1/2	red bell pepper, seeds and membrane removed, cut in fine julienne strips	1/2
1/2	yellow bell pepper, seeds and membrane removed, cut in fine julienne strips	1/2
2	Roma tomatoes, finely diced	2
1 recipe	Relish Niçoise (recipe follows)	1 recipe
4	4-oz. (113-g) Ahi tuna steaks salt and freshly ground black pepper to taste	4
2 Tbsp.	olive oil whole niçoise olives	30 mL

Arrange the mesclun greens in the centre of each of 4 plates. In a large bowl, combine the potato, green beans, red and yellow pepper and tomatoes. Toss with half the Relish Niçoise. Divide the salad among the plates and set aside.

Heat a medium sauté pan over high heat. Season the tuna with salt and pepper. When the pan is hot, reduce the heat to medium-high. Add the olive oil to the pan. When the oil is very hot, sear the tuna for 1 1/2 minutes per side.

Place the seared tuna on top of the salad, and top with more of the relish. Garnish each salad with whole niçoise olives.

Relish Niçoise

Makes about 1 cup (240 mL)

1/4 cup	white wine	60 mL
1 tsp.	Dijon mustard	5 mL
1 tsp.	grainy mustard	5 mL
1/2 cup	olive oil	120 mL
3	anchovies, chopped	3
3 Tbsp.	chopped niçoise olives	45 mL
2 Tbsp.	finely diced tomatoes	30 mL
1 Tbsp.	capers	15 mL
1 Tbsp.	chopped Italian parsley	15 mL
1 Tbsp.	chopped basil	15 mL
	salt and freshly ground black pepper to taste	

In a small bowl whisk together the white wine and the mustards. Still whisking, slowly add the olive oil. Stir in the anchovies, olives, tomatoes, capers, parsley and basil. Season with salt and pepper.

Summer Saffron Paella Salad

Like traditional paella, this salad cannot be made in small quantities. Make a pitcher of sangria and invite some friends over for a summer lunch. You could add mussels and/or scallops to this dish for a salad really packed with seafood.

Serves 8 to 10		Lesley Stowe
1/3 cup	olive oil	80 mL
4 tsp.	lemon juice	20 mL
1 Tbsp.	chopped fresh oregano	15 mL
1 Tbsp.	chopped fresh basil	15 mL
1 tsp.	freshly ground black pepper	5 mL
2 Tbsp.	finely minced garlic	30 mL
6	boneless skinless chicken breasts	6
24	prawn tails, peeled, the tips of the tails left on	24
1 1/2 cups	basmati rice	360 mL
2 1/2 cups	water	600 mL
1/4 tsp.	saffron filaments	1.2 mL

1 recipe	Vinaigrette	1 recipe
1/2	yellow bell pepper sliced in 1/4-inch (.6-cm) julienne	1/2
1/2	red bell pepper sliced in 1/4-inch (.6-cm) julienne	1/2
3/4 cup	green onions sliced into 1/4-inch (.6-cm) pieces	180 mL
1 cup	peeled, seeded, diced tomatoes	240 mL
1/2 cup	green olives cut into quarters	120 mL
	salt and black pepper to taste	

Mix the oil, lemon juice, oregano, basil, pepper and garlic in a shallow dish. Place the chicken in this mixture and marinate not more than 2 hours. Broil or grill the chicken breasts 4–5 minutes per side. Let cool and slice into 2- × 1/2-inch (5- × 1.2-cm) pieces. Set aside.

Bring a medium saucepan of water to a boil. Add the prawn tails and blanch for 1 minute, or just until the prawns turn opaque. Drain and rinse with cold water. Set aside.

Wash the basmati rice, drain and place in a medium saucepan with the water and saffron. Bring to a boil, then lower the heat to a slow simmer. Cover and cook 12–15 minutes, until all the water is absorbed. While the rice is cooking make the vinaigrette. Once the rice is cooked and still warm, toss with the vinaigrette. Add the peppers, green onions, tomatoes and olives. Toss well and add the chicken and prawns. Season to taste and serve.

Vinaigrette

Makes 1 cup (240 mL)

3/4 cup	extra-virgin olive oil	180 mL
1 Tbsp.	finely minced garlic	15 mL
1 Tbsp.	fresh oregano	15 mL
1 Tbsp.	fresh basil	15 mL
1/2 tsp.	turmeric	2.5 mL
1/2 tsp.	paprika	2.5 mL
3 Tbsp.	lemon juice	45 mL
	salt and black pepper to taste	

Heat the oil in a small saucepan, add the garlic and sauté for 1 minute. Remove from the heat and mix in the oregano, basil, turmeric, paprika, lemon juice and salt and pepper.

Clubhouse Chicken Salad with Green Goddess Dressing

Whatever happened to Green Goddess dressing? It was one of the first California food waves to make a splash. I just loved it, and would reach for the comfortably shaped bottle to pour over my salad, leaving the Catalina, Thousand Islands and Italian forlornly sitting on the table. I made the dressing occasionally in my early twenties, but somewhere, the spark died. I realize now that it was replaced by quiche, carrot cake and cheesecake—the romantic foodstuffs of the late 1970s. Now I have come to understand that the Goddess lives—especially when she's Green.

Serves 4		Karen Barnaby
1 cup	mayonnaise, homemade or store-bought	240 mL
1 cup	sour cream	240 mL
1	2-oz. (57-g) can anchovies, well drained	1
1 Tbsp.	lime juice	15 mL
3 Tbsp.	white wine vinegar	45 mL
1 Tbsp.	finely chopped fresh tarragon	15 mL
1/4 cup	finely chopped fresh chives	60 mL
1/2 cup	finely chopped parsley	120 mL
1/2 tsp.	salt	2.5 mL
1/2 tsp.	freshly ground black pepper	2.5 mL
1	large head romaine lettuce, washed, dried and torn into bite-size pieces	1
2 cups	freshly cooked chicken, cut into bite-size cubes	475 mL
3	large ripe tomatoes, cut into 1/2-inch (1.2-cm) cubes	3
1	avocado, pitted, peeled and cut into 1/4-inch (.6-cm) cubes	1
6	slices lean bacon, cooked until crisp and crumbled	6

To make the dressing, combine the mayonnaise, sour cream, anchovies, lime juice, vinegar, tarragon, chives, parsley, salt and pepper in the workbowl of a food processor or blender. Process until smooth. This dressing keeps for 2 weeks, covered and refrigerated.

Arrange the lettuce on a large platter. Scatter the chicken over the lettuce, then the tomatoes, avocado and bacon. Serve with the dressing on the side.

Lamb Salad with Crushed Peanuts & Lime Dressing

This is a variation on a traditional Thai salad known as lap. *The toasted rice powder binds the dressing to the ingredients. Serve with leaf lettuce and thinly sliced cucumber to wrap around the salad and convey it to waiting mouths.*

Serves 4		Karen Barnaby
2 Tbsp.	fresh lime juice	30 mL
1/4 tsp.	sugar	1.2 mL
1/4 tsp.	salt	1.2 mL
1 tsp.	fish sauce	5 mL
2–4	fresh Thai chiles, thinly sliced	2–4
1/4 cup	roasted, unsalted peanuts	60 mL
2	4-oz. (113-g) lamb loins	2
1 tsp.	vegetable oil	5 mL
	salt to taste	
2	green onions, sliced into thin rounds	2
1/2 cup	coarsely chopped cilantro	120 mL
1/2 cup	coarsely chopped mint	120 mL
1 Tbsp.	toasted rice powder (see below)	15 mL

Combine the lime juice, sugar, salt, fish sauce and chiles in a small bowl. Place the peanuts in a heavy plastic bag and crush with a rolling pin into pieces. You want to obtain different textures in the crushed peanuts, from pasty to crunchy. Set aside.

Cut the lamb loins in half lengthwise. Toss with the oil and salt. Heat a heavy, preferably cast-iron, pan over high heat. Place the lamb loins in the pan and sear on all sides until rare. You may do this on a barbecue if you wish. Remove from the heat and cool slightly. Place the green onions, cilantro and mint in a bowl. Thinly slice the lamb loins and add to the bowl. Add the dressing, peanuts and toasted rice powder. Toss well and serve immediately.

Note: To make toasted rice powder, dry-roast a cup (240 mL) of long grain glutinous rice (or plain long grain rice) in a frying pan, stirring constantly until dark brown. Pour into a bowl to cool. Grind to a coarse powder in a coffee grinder and store in a covered jar.

Lamb Loin with Seared Potato, Arugula & Red Wine Vinaigrette

The lamb loin is tender and succulent and should be cooked to medium-rare. The salad is served warm and can be used as a luncheon main course. This is a lovely spring dish: the potatoes add an earthy element and the vinaigrette a savoury counterpoint to the richness of the lamb.

Serves 4		Deb Connors
2	6-oz. (170-g) lamb loins	2
1/4 cup	red wine	60 mL
2 Tbsp.	balsamic vinegar	30 mL
1 tsp.	freshly ground black pepper	5 mL
2	cloves garlic, thinly sliced	2
1	bay leaf	1
1 tsp.	each chopped fresh thyme, oregano and parsley	5 mL
1/4 cup	olive oil	60 mL
6 Tbsp.	olive oil	90 mL
4	large shallots, coarsely chopped	4
8	small red potatoes, skin on, cut into 1-inch (2.5-cm) rounds	8
	salt and black pepper to taste	
2 oz.	pancetta, julienned	57 g
1 cup	arugula, loosely packed	240 mL
1 recipe	Red Wine Vinaigrette	1 recipe

Place the lamb in a non-reactive container. Combine the wine, vinegar, pepper, garlic, bay leaf, thyme, oregano, parsley, and the 1/4 cup (60 mL) olive oil. Pour over the lamb loin. Cover and marinate for 24 hours in the refrigerator.

Preheat the oven to 450°F (230°C). Remove the lamb from the marinade. Heat 2 Tbsp. (30 mL) of the olive oil in a sauté pan over medium-high heat. Sear the lamb loin on all sides, for 1–2 minutes. Finish the lamb in the oven for 4–5 minutes, depending on the thickness. Remove the lamb from the oven and allow to rest 5 minutes.

Heat the remaining 4 Tbsp. (60 mL) olive oil in a sauté pan. Fry the shallots until crisp. Remove and drain on paper towel. Set aside and keep warm.

Blanch the potato rounds in boiling water for 2 minutes. Pat dry. Reheat the olive oil used for the shallots and fry the potato rounds on both sides until brown. Remove the potatoes. Season with salt and pepper. Keep warm.

Using the same oil and sauté pan, lightly sauté the pancetta. Set aside and keep warm.

To serve, thinly slice the lamb loin and arrange in an overlapping semi-circle in the centre of each plate. Complete the circle with overlapped potato rounds. Garnish the centre with arugula and drizzle lightly with a little of the vinaigrette. Top with crisp shallots and pancetta bacon.

Red Wine Vinaigrette

Makes 2 cups (475 mL)

2 Tbsp.	olive oil	30 mL
1	small white onion, peeled and chopped	1
2 Tbsp.	chopped garlic	30 mL
4	tomatoes, coarsely chopped	4
4 Tbsp.	balsamic vinegar	60 mL
1 cup	red wine	240 mL
1/2 cup	olive oil	120 mL
	salt and freshly ground black pepper to taste	

Heat the 2 Tbsp. (30 mL) olive oil and sauté the onion and garlic over medium-high heat until it's soft and beginning to colour. Add the tomatoes and balsamic vinegar. Reduce the heat and cook 4–5 minutes, stirring often. Add the red wine and simmer for another 10 minutes over low heat. Place the contents of the sauté pan in a blender and purée. Push the mixture through a sieve, using a wooden spoon to extract all of the juices and some of the pulp. Place the strained mixture in a blender. With the blender running on high, slowly add the olive oil. Season with salt and pepper. Use at room temperature.

Soups

Sweet Corn & Vegetable Chowder with Red Pepper Purée

Use fresh corn when it's available. To add seafood to this chowder, lightly poach it and add it in the last few minutes of cooking. I like to add the fresh herbs at the very end so they retain their colour and bright flavours.

Serves 6 to 8		Deb Connors
1	red bell pepper	1
1 Tbsp.	olive oil	15 mL
1 Tbsp.	white wine	15 mL
	salt and freshly ground black pepper to taste	
3 Tbsp.	butter	45 mL
3	slices bacon, diced	3
2	cloves garlic, minced	2
1	small white onion, diced	1
1 cup	leeks, white parts only, washed and diced	240 mL
1 cup	diced carrots	240 mL
1/2 cup	diced celery	120 mL
2 Tbsp.	flour	30 mL
4 cups	chicken stock, heated	950 mL
2	large potatoes, peeled and diced	2
3 cups	fresh corn kernels (7 to 8 ears)	720 mL
2 cups	cream, heated	475 mL
	salt and freshly ground black pepper to taste	
	hot pepper sauce to taste	
1 Tbsp.	mixed fresh herbs, chopped	15 mL

Preheat the broiler. Place the red pepper on a tray directly under the broiler, using the top rack of your oven. Char it until the skin on all sides is blackened. Place the red pepper in a small bowl and cover tightly with plastic wrap for 10 minutes. When the pepper is cool enough to handle, remove the blackened skin. Discard the stem and seeds. Purée the roasted pepper in a blender, with the olive oil, white wine, salt and pepper. Set aside. This purée should be used at room temperature so as not to chill the soup.

Melt the butter in a heavy saucepan over medium-high heat. Add the bacon and sauté until browned, 2–3 minutes. Add the garlic, onion, leeks, carrots and celery. Cook, stirring often, another 2–3 minutes. Reduce the heat to low, add the flour and stir to make a roux. Cook for 4–5 minutes. Slowly whisk in the heated chicken stock. Add the potatoes and corn and simmer over medium-low heat for 20 minutes, until the vegetables are tender and the potatoes are cooked through. Add the heated cream and simmer 10 minutes more. Season with salt, pepper and hot sauce; stir in the fresh herbs.

Ladle the chowder into shallow bowls. Zigzag the red pepper purée across the top and serve.

Madrai Tomato Soup with Cumin & Coconut Milk

This combination sounds intriguing to some and bizarre to others, but it's one of the most popular soups in our store. This one is definitely worth trying.

Serves 8		Lesley Stowe
2 Tbsp.	butter	30 mL
1/3 cup	sesame seeds	80 mL
1 tsp.	ground cumin	5 mL
1 tsp.	mustard seed	5 mL
1 1/2 tsp.	cinnamon	7.5 mL
1 1/2 tsp.	ground coriander	7.5 mL
1 tsp.	salt	5 mL
1	13-oz. (370-mL) can coconut milk	1
6 cups	canned tomatoes	1.5 L
8 Tbsp.	yogurt	120 mL

Melt the butter in a medium cast-iron skillet. Sauté the sesame seeds, cumin, mustard seed, cinnamon and coriander over medium-high heat, stirring frequently, for 8–10 minutes, or until they give off a deeply toasted smell. Remove from the heat and add the salt. Combine the sautéed spice mixture with the coconut milk in a medium saucepan. Purée the tomatoes in a food mill to remove the seeds. Add the puréed tomatoes to the spiced coconut mixture and simmer very gently for 20 minutes. Taste for seasoning. Garnish with a tablespoon (15 mL) of yogurt swirled in the centre of each bowl.

azpacho

I can't think of a better way to spend a hot summer afternoon than to sit on a verandah drinking sangria and eating a cold bowl of gazpacho with a piece of soft focaccia. You can dress up this wonderful soup by garnishing it with some poached shrimp or a lobster tail.

Serves 4 to 6		Tamara Kourchenko
1	large green bell pepper, seeded	1
1	large red bell pepper, seeded	1
1/2	English or hot-house cucumber	1/2
1	medium white onion, peeled	1
1	stalk celery	1
3	cloves garlic, peeled	3
1 lb.	plum tomatoes	454 g
1/2	jalapeño pepper, seeds removed, or to taste	1/2
1/4 cup	cilantro leaves	60 mL
1/3 cup	red wine vinegar	80 mL
1/3 cup	extra-virgin olive oil	80 mL
	salt and black pepper to taste	
2 1/2 cups	tomato juice	600 mL

Cut all the vegetables into 1-inch (2.5-cm) pieces. Combine all the ingredients and purée thoroughly in a blender or food processor. If using a blender you may need to add a little bit of water or more tomato juice to purée it. Adjust the seasonings to taste; you may like a little more spice or vinegar. Depending on your preference, you may or may not strain the soup. At the restaurant we strain it; at home it's more casual, so I don't.

Tomato & Bread Soup

A very flavourful, rustic soup that turns day-old bread into a trip to southern Italy. If you have a special bottle of olive oil you have been saving, here is the recipe for it.

Serves 6		Caren McSherry-Valagao
1/3 cup	olive oil	80 mL
4	leeks, washed and sliced	4
4–5	cloves garlic, chopped	4–5
1/2 tsp.	hot pepper flakes	2.5 mL
4 1/4 cups	canned or fresh Italian plum tomatoes, diced	1 L
1/2 cup	white wine	120 mL
1 Tbsp.	sugar	15 mL
4 1/4 cups	chicken or vegetable stock	1 L
1	large loaf crusty Italian bread, day old	1
1 cup	fresh basil leaves	240 mL
	sea salt and freshly ground black pepper to taste	
6 Tbsp.	estate-quality, extra-virgin olive oil	90 mL
	freshly grated Parmesan cheese	

Heat the olive oil in a large pot. Add the leeks, garlic and pepper flakes and sauté over low heat until soft. Pass the tomatoes through a food mill or lightly pulse in the food processor. Add the tomatoes, wine and sugar to the pot. Bring to a boil and simmer for about 15 minutes. Add the stock and continue to simmer for another 10 minutes. Tear the bread into small pieces and add it to the soup. Stir over low heat for about 2 more minutes. The bread will begin to absorb the liquid. Remove from the heat, stir in the basil, adjust the seasonings to suit your taste and let the soup stand for about 5 minutes before serving.

To serve, ladle into bowls. Drizzle each bowl with 1 Tbsp. (15 mL) olive oil and sprinkle the top with Parmesan cheese.

Charred Vegetable Gazpacho

Grill the vegetables on the barbecue or indoors using a grill pan. Most chilled soups develop better flavour the second day but the chipotles—fire-smoked jalapeños—give this one a jolt from the start. For a sunny variation, use all yellow and green tomatoes and vegetables. Chipotles in a spicy sauce called adobo *are available in small cans in the Mexican foods section of supermarkets or in specialty food stores that have a "hot and spicy" section. Transfer leftover chipotles to a clean jar and refrigerate.*

Serves 0 to 8		Glenys Morgan
1	large red or sweet onion, peeled and cut into thick slices	1
1	red bell pepper, top and seeds removed, sliced into thick rings	1
1	yellow bell pepper, top and seeds removed, sliced into thick rings	1
6	tomatoes, halved	6
3	medium zucchini, quartered lengthwise and seeds removed	3
1	small eggplant, or 2 Japanese eggplants, thickly sliced	1
1/4 cup	olive oil	60 mL
1	English cucumber, cut into large chunks	1
1/4 cup	parsley or cilantro, coarse stems removed	60 mL
1 cup	loosely packed basil	240 mL
4 cups	tomato juice or spicy tomato vegetable juice, such as V-8	950 mL
2 tsp.	ground cumin	10 mL
1–2	chipotle chiles en adobo	1–2
	salt and freshly ground black pepper to taste	

Brush the onion, peppers, tomatoes, zucchini and eggplant with olive oil. Grill quickly over high heat. You want colour and flavour, but the vegetables should still be raw.

Working in batches, combine the grilled vegetables with the cucumber, herbs and tomato juice. Pulse until it's chunky but there are no large pieces. Add the cumin and chipotle to the last batch. Season with salt and pepper. Blend thoroughly and chill well. *Note:* As Karen Barnaby suggests, if it's not smoky enough, add a couple of drops of natural hickory smoke liquid. It contains only water and hickory smoke and is available at grocery stores.

Roasted Garlic & Brie Soup

This creamy soup is wonderful served with crusty bread and red wine. The better quality Brie you use, the richer the soup will be. If you wish, you can garnish it with croutons.

Serves 0 to 8		Tamara Kourchenko
2	heads garlic, roasted (see page 7)	2
2 Tbsp.	butter, unsalted	30 mL
1	medium white onion, thinly sliced	1
2	medium leeks, white part only, washed and thinly sliced	2
1/2 tsp.	salt	2.5 mL
1/2 tsp.	pepper	2.5 mL
1 cup	dry vermouth or white wine	240 mL
3/4 lb.	russet potatoes, peeled and quartered	340 g
6 cups	unsalted chicken stock	1.5 L
2 cups	heavy cream	475 mL
1/3 cup	grated Parmesan cheese	80 mL
4 oz.	Brie cheese	113 g

Squeeze the garlic cloves from the husks and set aside.

In a large pot, melt the butter and add the onion, leeks, salt and pepper. Cook over low heat, stirring occasionally, until the vegetables are soft but not brown, about 10 minutes. Add the vermouth or wine and reduce until almost all the liquid has evaporated. Add the potatoes, roasted garlic and chicken stock, and simmer slowly until the potatoes are very soft. Add the cream and both cheeses and stir until they melt. Purée the soup and strain. Check the seasonings. Bring back to a boil before serving.

Asparagus & Aged White Cheddar Soup

When asparagus is in season, our kitchen is in a frenzy, using it in as many ways as possible. This is one of the staff's favourite soups. The addition of a good aged cheddar adds some body and elegance.

Serves 8		Lesley Stowe
5 Tbsp.	butter	75 mL
1	small yellow onion, finely diced	1
1	leek, well washed, finely diced	1
	salt and black pepper to taste	
1 lb.	asparagus, approximately 1 1/2 inches (3.8 cm) of the stem removed	454 g
5 1/2 cups	water	1.3 L
6 Tbsp.	flour	90 mL
1 1/3 cups	hot milk	320 mL
1/2 lb.	aged white Cheddar cheese, grated	225 g

Melt 2 Tbsp. (30 mL) of the butter in a large heavy saucepan and sauté the onion and leek over medium heat until soft. Season with salt and pepper.

Reserve 1/3 of the asparagus for garnish. Chop the remaining asparagus into 1-inch (2.5-cm) pieces. Add the asparagus and water to the leeks and onions. Bring to a boil, then simmer until the asparagus is tender, 5–8 minutes.

Purée the mixture in several batches in the blender. At this point you may strain the liquid through a sieve, but it is not absolutely necessary. Chop the reserved asparagus into 1/4-inch (.6-cm) pieces and set aside.

In a large heavy saucepan, melt the remaining 3 Tbsp. (45 mL) of butter. Stir in the flour and cook over medium-low heat for 5–10 minutes. Whisk in the hot milk until the mixture is smooth. Bring to a boil to thicken. Add the asparagus purée and the chopped asparagus. Bring to a boil and simmer 5–10 minutes, or until the asparagus is just tender. Remove from the heat and stir in the Cheddar cheese. Do not boil it once the cheese is added or the soup could curdle. Check for seasoning and add salt and pepper if desired.

Winter Squash Soup with Apple Cider & Thyme

Winter squashes are the ones with a hard skin, but this doesn't mean that you can't make this soup in the fall, when the first squashes come out and are very sweet. I like using an assortment of squashes, but when making small amounts it's easier to use just one variety. Choose some of the intriguing sweet varieties like Banana, Honeydew or Hubbard squash. Butternut squash works very well too and it's more readily available.

Serves 6 to 8		Tamara Kourchenko
4 Tbsp.	unsalted butter	60 mL
4 Tbsp.	thinly sliced white onion	60 mL
1 lb.	squash, peeled and cut into 1-inch (2.5-cm) pieces	454 g
1	medium carrot, peeled and cut into 1-inch (2.5-cm) pieces	1
1/2 cup	white wine	120 mL
1 cup	apple cider or natural apple juice	240 mL
7 cups	unsalted chicken stock	1.7 L
1 Tbsp.	chopped fresh thyme	15 mL
	salt and black pepper to taste	
	sour cream	
	chopped parsley	

Melt the butter in a large pot. Add the onion and cook over low heat until translucent and soft. Add the squash, carrot and white wine and cook until reduced by half. Pour in the apple cider or juice and continue reducing until almost all the liquid has evaporated. Add the chicken stock and thyme, salt and pepper and simmer slowly until all the vegetables are very soft.

Cool slightly, purée and strain. Serve garnished with a small dollop of sour cream and some chopped parsley.

Lesley Stowe

A food fiend from a young age, my earliest recollection of a desire to cook was at the age of twelve when I locked my family out of the kitchen and proceeded to make a meal around Boeuf Chausseur and Apple Charlotte. The fire was lit, but it wasn't until I spent a summer backpacking around Europe and a day in the kitchen of La Varenne in Paris that I knew this was my calling.

After completion of my BA in Art History, I was back in Paris to spend a year cooking, eating and learning everything I could about food. Upon returning to Vancouver, I started a small cooking school in the Wise Owl Kitchen Shop, followed by a time managing Salt Box Cooking and Catering.

In 1990 it was time to launch out on my own. Not confident that there was enough catering to keep us bubbling all year, I decided that the desserts served in restaurants needed some help and "Death By Chocolate," that now famous concoction, was born. After five years of serving the restaurant industry and tired of not being able to find quality specialty foods, I opened Lesley Stowe Fine Foods, a first of its kind in Vancouver, where customers can choose from myriad cheeses, olive oils, vinegars, coffees, breads, desserts, entrées and cookbooks.

More than just retailing food, I want to educate and inspire the public by conducting tastings, workshops and classes, and providing them with quality ingredients for their own creations. In addition to teaching at my own location, I have done workshops in Calgary and recently hosted a cooking school session at Umberto's Villa Delia in Tuscany with my husband Douglas.

What I find most exciting about cooking today is the availability of ingredients and the vast array of cuisines we are experimenting with as a result. I believe this book is a reflection of that and hope you will enjoy cooking from it and sharing your results with family and friends.

White Bean Soup with Roasted Garlic & Rosemary Oil

I am crazy about white beans and they lend themselves so well to flavours like garlic and rosemary. A real comfort dish, you can make a dinner of this soup with a good crusty bread and a chunk of Parmesan.

Serves 8		Lesley Stowe
3 Tbsp.	olive oil	45 mL
2	large onions, peeled and coarsely chopped	2
2	medium carrots, peeled and coarsely chopped	2
7 cups	chicken or vegetable stock	1.7 L
1 cup	cannellini beans, soaked overnight and drained	240 mL
8	medium cloves garlic, roasted 15–20 minutes until soft (see page 7)	8
1	bay leaf	1
1 1/2 tsp.	salt	7.5 mL
1/2 tsp.	freshly ground black pepper	2.5 mL
1 Tbsp.	lemon juice	15 mL
1/4 cup	freshly grated Parmesan cheese	60 mL
1/4 cup	finely chopped parsley	60 mL
1/4 cup	rosemary oil	60 mL

Heat the oil in a 6-quart (6-L) soup pot. Sauté the onions over low heat for about 5 minutes, stirring occasionally. Add the carrots and sauté another 3 minutes. Add the stock, beans, garlic and bay leaf. Partially cover and simmer for about 1 hour, until the beans are tender. Remove the bay leaf. Purée the soup and return it to the pot. Bring to a simmer and add salt, pepper and lemon juice. Taste for seasoning. Ladle the soup into bowls, sprinkle with cheese and parsley and drizzle with rosemary oil.

Smoky Bean, Bacon & Prawn Soup

Don't shy away from making a bean soup from scratch. Cannellini—baby lima beans in the market—cook quickly in this short-form method even without presoaking. Grilled prawns add another layer of smoky flavour (or substitute shredded smoked chicken).

Serves 6 to 8		Glenys Morgan
1 cup	dried cannellini or other white bean, sorted and rinsed	240 mL
4	slices double-smoked bacon	4
1	large onion, peeled and coarsely chopped	1
2	large carrots, peeled and coarsely chopped	2
4	cloves garlic, peeled	4
1	sprig fresh rosemary, or 1 tsp. (5 mL) dried rosemary leaves	1
1	small red chile, crushed, or 1/2 tsp. (2.5 mL) red pepper flakes	1
1 oz.	bourbon or cognac	30 mL
4 cups	homemade chicken stock, vegetable stock or water	950 mL
2 Tbsp.	butter	30 mL
	salt and freshly ground black pepper to taste	
18–24	prawns, shells removed (allow at least 3 per bowl)	18–24
2 Tbsp.	olive oil	30 mL
1/2 cup	grated Parmesan cheese	120 mL
	finely chopped parsley	

Place the beans in a large heavy pot and cover with water. Bring to a boil and drain, discarding the cooking water. Rinse the beans. In the same pot on medium-high heat, let the bacon warm and brown slightly. Add the onion, carrots and garlic. Mix well and let the vegetables cook until softened and slightly golden.

Add the beans, rosemary and chile to the pot. (Do not add salt, or the beans will not soften.) Pour in the bourbon or cognac and enough chicken stock to cover the beans by 1 inch (2.5 cm). Bring to a boil, then reduce the heat and simmer, uncovered, until the beans are tender, about 45–60 minutes. Check frequently to see if the stock needs to be replenished. Use water if necessary.

Drain and reserve the broth. Remove the rosemary sprig. Purée the bean mixture in the food processor or with a hand blender, adding only small additions of the broth as necessary. Working with too much liquid brings out a starchy taste and texture; it's better to add the liquid back in at the end.

Reheat the soup gently and adjust the thickness with a little stock or water if too thick. It will also thicken as it cooks. Add the butter when the soup is warm and season with salt and pepper. Let the soup simmer while preparing the prawns.

Note: Don't substitute canned or cube stock for homemade when cooking the beans. The high salt content will keep the beans from softening. If necessary, cook the beans with water and add the commercial stock after puréeing the beans.

Heat a small skillet or grill. Toss the prawns with the olive oil to coat. Sear very quickly until just opaque and pink. The prawns may be chopped into pieces if desired. Stir the Parmesan cheese into the soup. Ladle the soup into bowls. Garnish with the prawns in the centre of each bowl and a sprinkling of parsley to brighten the flavour. Serve with a loaf of crusty bread.

Crème de la Pork & Bean

A creamy white bean soup, topped with basil oil and crisp bacon—or, if you prefer, prosciutto.

Serves 4		Mary Mackay
1 1/4 cups	dry navy beans	300 mL
2 cups	water	475 mL
1/4 lb.	bacon, diced (about 4 slices)	113 g
1/3 cup	finely diced onion	80 mL
2	cloves garlic, minced	2
1/3 cup	finely chopped leeks	80 mL
1/3 cup	finely chopped celery	80 mL
2 tsp.	ground cumin seed	10 mL
1 tsp.	salt	5 mL
6 cups	vegetable stock or water	1.5 L
1 cup	whipping cream	240 mL
4 tsp.	finely chopped fresh basil	20 mL
4 tsp.	olive oil	20 mL
	cracked black peppercorns to taste	

Soak the navy beans in the water overnight.

In a large, heavy pot over medium-high heat, cook half the bacon until almost crisp. Add the onion, garlic, leeks, celery, cumin and salt and sauté until the vegetables are soft, about 5 minutes. Add the stock or water to the pot.

Drain the navy beans through a sieve and rinse them under cold water. Add them to the pot. Bring to a boil, lower the heat to medium and simmer for 1 hour. Cool the soup until it's safe to transfer to a blender.

Purée the soup, then pass it through a fine sieve. Return to the pot over medium heat and stir in the whipping cream. Adjust the seasoning with salt if necessary. Keep warm over low heat.

Fry the remaining bacon until crisp and drain on paper towel. Crush the basil in a mortar and pestle, or in a small bowl with a soupspoon, then add the olive oil and stir. Ladle the soup into 4 bowls. Drizzle 1 tsp. (5 mL) basil oil on the top of each serving. Garnish with crisp bacon bits and cracked black peppercorns.

Thai Lime & Chicken Soup

This fragrant soup is light and refreshing. It embodies several elements of Thai cooking that I adore—fresh lime and ginger, the combination of cilantro and basil and a little heat. A small amount of Thai fish sauce brings a roundness and depth to the soup. It is easy to find in Asian food shops, but if you can't find it, don't worry—the soup is delicious without it.

Serves 5		Margaret Chisholm
1/2 lb.	boneless skinless chicken breast	225 g
4 cups	chicken stock	950 mL
1/3 cup	soy sauce	80 mL
2 Tbsp.	Thai fish sauce (optional)	30 mL
1	carrot, thinly sliced on the diagonal	1
1/2 cup	snow peas, cut in 1-inch (2.5-cm) pieces	120 mL
3 oz.	rice noodles or bean threads	85 g
2 tsp.	grated fresh ginger	10 mL
1	clove garlic, chopped	1
1/2 tsp.	Thai red chili paste	2.5 mL
1 tsp.	sugar	5 mL
1/4 cup	green onions	60 mL
3 Tbsp.	cilantro	45 mL
2 Tbsp.	Thai or sweet basil	30 mL
2 Tbsp.	freshly squeezed lime juice	30 mL

Poach the chicken in the chicken stock until it's cooked through. Remove the chicken and reserve the stock. When the chicken is cool, cut it into 1/4-inch (1.2-cm) slices. Combine the soy and fish sauce and marinate the chicken for 10 minutes or more.

Heat the reserved stock to a simmer, add the carrot slices and simmer for about 4 minutes, or until tender. Add the snow peas, rice noodles, ginger, garlic, chili paste and sugar. Simmer for 2 minutes.

Just before serving, add the chicken and its marinade, green onions, cilantro, basil and lime juice. Serve immediately.

Yucatan Chicken & Chile Soup

This hugely flavourful soup hails from the Yucatan in Mexico.
The chipotle chiles are actually smoked jalapeño peppers. I use
the smoky adobo sauce that the chiles are preserved in to baste
the chicken. It is quite spicy, so sissies beware.

Serves 8		Caren McSherry-Valagao
3	whole boneless skinless chicken breasts	3
1	small can chipotle chiles in adobo sauce	1
15	medium Roma tomatoes	15
2	heads garlic, roasted (see page 7)	2
2 Tbsp.	corn oil	30 mL
1	large white onion, diced	1
8 cups	chicken stock	2 L
1/2 tsp.	Mexican oregano	2.5 mL
1/2	bunch chopped cilantro	1/2
2	fresh limes, cut into quarters	2
1	small bag plain tortilla chips	1
1/2 cup	sour cream	120 mL

Lay the chicken flat on your work surface. Brush it lightly with the adobo
sauce from the canned chiles. Chop 2 whole chiles and set aside. Reserve the
remaining chiles for another use.

Grill, broil, or barbecue the chicken on both sides until browned and cooked
through. Set aside. Place the tomatoes in an ungreased cast-iron frying pan and
dry-roast them on medium-high heat until they become blackened all over.
Shake the pan at intervals. Set aside to cool. Squeeze the pulp from the roasted
garlic and set aside.

Heat the corn oil in a large pot, add the onion and sauté for 3 minutes, or until
soft. Place the tomatoes in the bowl of a food processor and purée. Add it to the
onions along with the roasted garlic, chopped chipotle chiles, stock, oregano and
cilantro. Simmer for 20 minutes.

To serve, julienne the chicken and place some in the bottom of each serving
bowl. Ladle the hot soup over top. Give each bowl a squeeze of lime and drop
the wedge into the soup. Garnish with a few crushed tortilla chips and a
spoonful of sour cream.

Entrées

Sautéed Scallops over Thai-Spiced Risotto

This classic risotto of Arborio rice, butter and Parmesan cheese is enriched with Thai red curry coconut broth. The Thai spices in this recipe can be found in most Asian food markets. If these ingredients are not readily available, you can substitute lemon zest for lemon grass, lime zest for kaffir lime leaves, and curry powder for red curry paste.

Serves 4		*Mary Mackay*
1 2/3 cup	coconut milk	400 mL
4 cups	chicken stock or water	950 mL
1	stalk lemon grass, coarsely chopped	1
2	kaffir lime leaves	2
2 tsp.	red curry paste	10 mL
3 Tbsp.	unsalted butter	45 mL
3 Tbsp.	finely diced onion	45 mL
2 oz.	shiitake mushrooms, thinly sliced (6 large)	57 g
1 tsp.	minced ginger	5 mL
2 cups	Arborio rice	475 mL
2 Tbsp.	lime juice	30 mL
1/4 cup	grated Parmesan cheese	60 mL
3 Tbsp.	chopped fresh cilantro	45 mL
	salt and black pepper to taste	
1 lb.	sea scallops, foot removed	454 g
	lime wedges	

Place the coconut milk, stock or water, lemon grass, kaffir lime leaves and curry paste in a medium-sized pot and bring to a boil. Remove from the heat and let sit for 15 minutes. Pass the stock through a strainer, return to the pot, and bring back to a simmer.

Melt 1 Tbsp. (15 mL) of the butter in a large heavy pot over medium-high heat. Sauté the onion, mushrooms and ginger in the butter until soft. Stir in the rice. Add 1/2 cup (120 mL) of the hot stock and stir until the liquid is absorbed. Continue adding stock, 1/2 cup (120 mL) at a time, stirring continuously. When all the stock is absorbed and the rice is creamy, stir in the lime juice, cheese and cilantro. Adjust the seasoning with salt and pepper. Cover to keep warm.

Season the scallops with salt and pepper. Melt the remaining 2 Tbsp. (30 mL) of butter in a large non-stick frying pan over high heat. When the butter is hot, arrange the scallops in the pan, evenly spaced. Brown the scallops 1–2 minutes on each side.

To assemble, divide the risotto evenly into 4 bowls. Top with the sautéed scallops and garnish with lime.

Grilled Prawns & Prosciutto with Basil Sauce

The salty sweet of the prosciutto and prawns are a wonderful flavour combination, but the basil sauce adds a whole new dimension.

Serves 6		Caren McSherry-Valagao
2	large shallots	2
2 cups	firmly packed fresh basil leaves	475 mL
2–3	cloves garlic, peeled	2–3
3 Tbsp.	pine nuts	45 mL
2 tsp.	balsamic vinegar	10 mL
1/2 cup	extra-virgin olive oil	120 mL
	sea salt and freshly ground black pepper to taste	
18	large prawns, head off, tail on	18
9	thin slices of prosciutto, preferably Italian	9

To roast the shallots, peel and rub lightly with olive oil. Place them in a garlic roaster or wrap in foil and bake at 325°F (165°C) for about 40 minutes, or until they are soft and golden in colour.

Place the roasted shallots, basil, garlic, pine nuts and vinegar in a blender or the bowl of a food processor and purée until the mixture is smooth, scraping down the sides of the bowl one or two times. With the motor running, slowly pour in the oil. The sauce will thicken slightly. Season with salt and pepper.

Dry the prawns thoroughly. Cut the prosciutto in half lengthwise and wrap one piece around the body of each prawn. Rub the wrapped prawn with a scant amount of olive oil. Heat a barbecue or grill to high. Cook the prawns until they are bright pink, turning only once. This should take about 3–4 minutes. Serve hot off the grill with the basil sauce.

Coriander Prawns with Sun-Dried Tomato Coulis & Pineapple Mango Relish

This dish makes a particularly great summer meal. The prawns can easily be done on an outside grill or barbecue. The marinade adds a bright but subtle flavour to the prawns. The pineapple mango relish adds a light and refreshing accent. Everything can be prepared ahead and it takes just minutes to cook the prawns.

Serves 6		Deb Connors
48	prawns (16–20 per lb./454 g)	48
2 Tbsp.	lemon juice	30 mL
2 Tbsp.	ground coriander	30 mL
1 Tbsp.	freshly ground black pepper	15 mL
1 tsp.	ground cumin	5 mL
1/4 tsp.	turmeric	1.2 mL
2 Tbsp.	Italian parsley, chopped	30 mL
1/2 cup	olive oil	120 mL
1 recipe	Pineapple Mango Relish	1 recipe
1 recipe	Sun-Dried Tomato Coulis	1 recipe

Arrange the prawns on a flat surface in rows of 8 with the tails facing in the same direction. Push 2 wooden skewers through each row of prawns, spacing the skewers 1 inch (2.5 cm) apart. Space the prawns 1/2 inch (1.2 cm) apart. Place in a shallow dish.

Process the lemon juice, coriander, pepper, cumin, turmeric, and parsley for 30 seconds in a blender. With the blender running, slowly add the olive oil. Pour the marinade over the prawns and marinate 2–4 hours. Preheat the grill. Cook the prawns for 2 minutes on each side until they are opaque and just cooked through.

Place a portion of Pineapple Mango Relish in the centre of each serving plate. Centre a prawn skewer on the relish and drizzle a little Sun-Dried Tomato Coulis over the prawns.

Pineapple Mango Relish

1/2 cup	mango, peeled and pitted, fine dice	120 mL
1/2 cup	finely diced pineapple	120 mL
2 Tbsp.	finely diced red bell pepper	30 mL
1/2	jalapeño pepper, minced	1/2
1/2	red onion, cut in fine julienne strips	1/2
2 Tbsp.	fresh lime juice	30 mL
1 Tbsp.	olive oil	15 mL
1 1/2 Tbsp.	finely chopped cilantro	22.5 mL
1 Tbsp.	honey	15 mL
	salt and freshly ground black pepper to taste	

In a large bowl combine the mango, pineapple, red pepper, jalapeño pepper, and red onion. Stir in the lime juice, olive oil, cilantro, honey and salt and pepper.

Sun-Dried Tomato Coulis

2 oz.	sun-dried tomatoes	57 g
3 Tbsp.	olive oil	45 mL
4	shallots, peeled and sliced	4
1/4 tsp.	salt	1.2 mL
1/4 tsp.	freshly ground black pepper	1.2 mL
1/2 cup	white wine	120 mL
1/2 cup	chicken stock	120 mL

Soak the sun-dried tomatoes in hot water for 5 minutes and drain. Heat the olive oil in a sauté pan over medium heat and cook the shallots for 2–3 minutes. Add the drained tomatoes, salt and pepper, white wine and chicken stock. Bring to a boil, reduce the heat and simmer 3–4 minutes. Purée in a blender at high speed. If the coulis is too thick, thin with a little more white wine. The coulis may be made 2 days ahead and refrigerated. Bring to room temperature before serving.

Salmon Bake with Sour Cream, Bacon & New Red Potatoes

When an idea strikes, it is usually a combination of flavours or ingredients. In this case, I had the title "King Salmon Bake" spinning around in my head before I knew what it was. What it turned out to be was a cozy combination of salmon, cheesey spinach and potatoes that became one of the best sellers in the history of the Fish House in Stanley Park. King salmon is the U.S. name for spring salmon.

Serves 4		Karen Barnaby
1 lb.	small red potatoes	454 g
1 lb.	spinach, stems removed, washed and drained	454 g
1 Tbsp.	unsalted butter, melted	15 mL
1 cup	shredded, extra-old white Cheddar cheese or Asiago	240 mL
1	clove garlic, minced	1
1/2 tsp.	salt	2.5 mL
	salt and freshly ground black pepper to taste	
1 Tbsp.	unsalted butter	15 mL
4	6-oz. (170-g) skinless, boneless salmon fillets	4
2 tsp.	lemon juice	10 mL
8	slices good-quality bacon	8
4 Tbsp.	sour cream, heaping	60 mL
1 Tbsp.	minced chives	15 mL

Preheat the oven to 350°F (175°C).

Cook the potatoes in boiling water until just tender, approximately 20–25 minutes. Drain and cool.

Place the spinach in a large pot, turn the heat to high and cover with a lid. Steam until it wilts, turning it over occasionally. Transfer to a large plate and spread out to cool. When cool, squeeze into small balls with your hands to remove the water. Finely chop and place in a bowl. Add the melted butter, cheese, garlic and salt. Mix well. The potatoes and the spinach mixture may be prepared up to a day in advance. Cover and refrigerate.

Slice the potatoes into 1/4-inch-thick (.6-cm) slices and arrange in slightly overlapping rows in an 8- × 11 1/2-inch (20- × 29-cm) baking dish. Season well with salt and pepper and dot with half the 1 Tbsp. (15 mL) butter. Divide the spinach mixture into 4 equal portions, flatten each into an elongated patty and place one in each quarter of the baking dish over the potatoes. Place a salmon fillet over each patty of spinach, sprinkle with the lemon juice, dot with the remaining butter and season with salt and pepper. Cover snugly with foil and bake for 20–30 minutes, until the salmon is cooked through.

While the salmon is cooking, fry the bacon over medium heat until crisp. Drain on paper towels and crumble when cool. When the salmon is done, lift each portion onto heated individual plates or leave in the baking dish. Top each piece of salmon with a dollop of sour cream. Sprinkle the bacon and chives over the sour cream and serve immediately.

Sweet BBQ Salmon, Rivers Inlet Style

I learned this technique one summer when I worked as a cook in a sports fishing camp on the central coast of B.C. In the last few years I have introduced it to many students and customers who have responded with rave reviews. Here I pair it with a delicious compound butter. Fennel Mashed Potatoes (page 126) is a great accompaniment.

Serves 6		Margaret Chisholm
1/4 cup	brown sugar	60 mL
2 Tbsp.	coarse salt	30 mL
1/2 tsp.	dry mustard	2.5 mL
2 1/2 lbs.	skinless salmon fillets	1.1 kg
1 recipe	Sun-Dried Tomato, Caper & Dill Butter	1 recipe

Mix the brown sugar, salt and dry mustard together. Sprinkle onto both sides of the salmon fillets. Marinate in a non-reactive dish for 4 to 5 hours, turning occasionally. The next step is very important: rinse the salmon well under cold running water.

Preheat the barbecue or grill and oil lightly. Grill the salmon for approximately 4 minutes per side, or until the fish is barely firm. Just before serving, unwrap the chilled butter and cut into 1/2-inch (1.2-cm) nuggets. Place on the hot fish and serve.

Note: When barbecuing a large, thick chunk of salmon, you can leave the skin on and grill it skin side up for a few minutes to mark the salmon nicely with grill marks, then turn it over and complete the cooking with the skin side down. The skin will become charred, then it will separate easily and the salmon can be lifted off, leaving the skin behind.

Sun-Dried Tomato, Caper & Dill Butter

Makes a 3-inch (7.5-cm) log

2 Tbsp.	very finely chopped sun-dried tomatoes	30 mL
2 tsp.	finely chopped capers	10 mL
1 Tbsp.	finely chopped dill	15 mL
5 Tbsp.	unsalted butter, softened to room temperature	75 mL

Place all ingredients in a small bowl and beat very well with a wooden spoon. Scrape the mixture onto a piece of wax paper or parchment. Fold the paper over the mixture and roll up into a 3-inch (7.5-cm) tube. Chill well.

Seared Salmon Fillet with Scallions, Portobello Mushrooms & Dark Ginger Sauce

Everyone is looking for an innovative way to serve salmon. This Asian-flavoured dish is rich in taste, not calories. You can serve it to family or at your most elegant dinner party. Try it with wasabi mashed potatoes for a real taste treat.

Serves 8		Lesley Stowe
2	bunches green onions	2
10 oz.	portobello mushrooms	285 g
2 Tbsp.	peanut oil	30 mL
2 Tbsp.	sesame seeds	30 mL
2 Tbsp.	peanut oil	30 mL
2 tsp.	sesame oil	10 mL
1	2-inch (5-cm) piece fresh ginger, peeled and cut in julienne strips	1
2 Tbsp.	water	30 mL
4 tsp.	soy sauce	20 mL
1 tsp.	cornstarch	5 mL
1/4 cup	brown sugar	60 mL
1/2 tsp.	freshly ground black pepper	2.5 mL
3 lbs.	salmon fillets, skin removed, cut into 8 pieces	1.4 kg
1/2 cup	peanut oil	120 mL
1/4 cup	soy sauce	60 mL
1/4 cup	water	60 mL

Clean the green onions, discarding all but 3 inches (7.5 cm) of the greens. Cut into 1 1/2-inch (4-cm) pieces on a 45-degree angle. Sauté the mushrooms in 2 Tbsp. (30 mL) peanut oil. Set aside. Toast the sesame seeds in a small heavy skillet over medium heat until brown. Remove to a small bowl.

Heat the remaining 2 Tbsp. (30 mL) peanut oil and the sesame oil in the small skillet with the ginger. Add the green onions and stir-fry for 30 seconds, or until tender. Add the water, soy sauce and cornstarch, and cook until the sauce has thickened. Add the mushrooms.

Mix the sugar and pepper in a large bowl. Dip one side of each salmon fillet into the mixture and place on a platter. Heat the 1/2 cup (120 mL) peanut oil in a large, non-stick frying pan over medium-high heat. Add the salmon and cook for about 3 minutes, until the bottom is browned and caramelized. Pour the soy sauce and water into the skillet. Cover and continue cooking for about 3–5 minutes, until the fish is glazed and just opaque throughout. The salmon can be cooked in batches, draining the pan and adding more peanut oil, soy sauce and water between batches.

To serve, rewarm the green onion and mushroom mixture by stirring over medium-high heat. Transfer the salmon to individual plates. Spoon the onions and mushrooms over the salmon and sprinkle with the toasted sesame seeds. Serve immediately.

Pan-Roasted Chilean Sea Bass on Braised Red Cabbage

The fantastic flavour and, firm, white flesh of Chilean sea bass contrast with the bright purple cabbage and its slightly tangy taste. This is a comforting and elegant dish for the fall and winter months, when fresh Chilean sea bass is available. In spring or summer, you can substitute fresh halibut.

Serves 6		Tamara Kourchenko

For the braised cabbage:

4 Tbsp.	butter, unsalted	60 mL
1	apple, quartered and thinly sliced	1
1 cup	white onion, thinly sliced	240 mL
2 lbs.	red cabbage, cored and thinly sliced	900 g
1 1/2 cups	red wine	360 mL
1 cup	apple cider vinegar	240 mL
2–3 cups	unsalted chicken stock	475–720 mL
	salt and black pepper to taste	

In a large saucepan melt the butter. Add the apple and onion and cook over medium heat, stirring occasionally, until the onion is soft. Add the cabbage and stir. Deglaze the pan with the red wine. Add the vinegar and 2 cups of chicken stock. Cover and cook over low heat, stirring occasionally. The cabbage can also be cooked, covered, in a 350°F (175°C) oven. The cooking time will vary, depending on your stove, but it should take 45 minutes to 1 hour. When it's done, the cabbage will not be crunchy, and almost all the liquid will have evaporated. If the cabbage gets too dry and starts sticking, lower the heat and add a little more chicken stock. Season with salt and pepper and maybe a little more vinegar, depending on your taste.

For the fennel sauce:

4 Tbsp.	unsalted butter	60 mL
1 cup	white onion, thinly sliced	240 mL
10 oz.	fennel, cored and thinly sliced	285 g
	salt and black pepper to taste	
2 cups	dry white wine	475 mL
6 cups	unsalted chicken stock	1.5 L
1/2 cup	heavy cream	120 mL

Melt the butter in a medium saucepan. Add the onion and fennel. Season with a little salt and pepper and cook very slowly over low heat, stirring occasionally, until the vegetables are very tender and soft, but not brown. This is the most important step of the sauce, since this is when the vegetables develop their flavour and become sweet. It is very important not to rush this.

Once the vegetables are soft, add the white wine and simmer until almost all the liquid has evaporated. Add the chicken stock and reduce by half. Let cool slightly, purée and strain back into the same pot.

Add the cream and simmer until the sauce thickens enough to coat the back of a spoon. Check for seasoning and add salt and pepper if desired.

To assemble:

4 Tbsp.	vegetable oil	60 mL
6	Chilean sea bass fillets, about 6 oz. (170 g) each	6
	salt and black pepper to taste	
4 Tbsp.	extra-virgin olive oil	60 mL
9 oz.	spinach leaves, washed	255 g
	salt and black pepper to taste	
	braised cabbage	
	fennel sauce	

Preheat the oven to 450°F (230°C).

Preheat the vegetable oil in 1 or 2 pans large enough to hold 6 pieces of fish and just barely cover the bottom. Season the fish with salt and pepper. When the pan is smoking hot, sear the fish on one side. If the pan is not hot enough, the fish will stick. When the fillets are golden brown on one side, turn them over and place the pans in the oven for about 5–7 minutes. When the fish is done it will feel firm and flake slightly.

Heat up another pan and add the extra-virgin olive oil. Add the spinach, season with salt and pepper, and toss until it wilts slightly.

Place the spinach in the centre of each plate. Arrange some red cabbage on top of the spinach, and the fish on the cabbage. Drizzle some fennel sauce on the plate around the spinach and pass the remaining sauce separately.

Deb Connors

*D*eb Connors hated food. As a kid in Grand Falls, Newfoundland, she had to be paid to eat. Paid, bribed, threatened—whatever worked. "Nothing tasted good," she recalls. "It's different now, but in those days (let's just say it was awhile ago), everything had to come 100 miles by boat and 300 miles by truck to reach us. There was almost no local farming, so we didn't have a lot of variety or quality. Salt beef in a bucket of brine—horrid. Salt cod—you'd spend a long time cooking it up, and when it was done, you'd think, 'Why?' I didn't learn to think of food in a positive way."

Today, as head chef at Aqua Riva, things have obviously changed for Connors. Food is her obsession. It seems that young Deb never hated food after all—she just wanted quality.

The turning point for Connors came when, at age nineteen, she moved across the country to the Comox Valley on Vancouver Island. Soon, she was making up for lost time. In her huge garden, she grew everything from raspberries and strawberries to peanuts and melons. The yard was home to chickens, rabbits and a goat. A friend had a catering business, which further piqued Connor's interest. "I realized I knew almost nothing about food and cooking," she says. "I decided to work in a restaurant." It's a mark of her determination that she was able to talk her way into a job at Courtenay's famous Old House dining room.

The Old House was where I served my apprenticeship, under British chef Andrew Howarth. Later came the usual assortment of jobs most experienced chefs look back on with bemusement. At one Vancouver Island spot, Connors was cooking New Year's Day brunch while bailiffs were loading the kitchen equipment and supplies onto a truck. "I had to negotiate with them to get enough eggs to feed 80 customers," Connors recalls ruefully.

She arrived in Vancouver in 1985 to help open up Joe Fortes. A year later, Andrew Howarth came back into the picture. Now chef at the Salmon House on the Hill, he was dragging his heels about hiring a new sous-chef. That's because Howarth had no intention of hiring anyone but Connors, whether Connors liked it or not. "He tricked me," she laughs. "I said I didn't want the job." "Just come for dinner," he said. "By the end of dinner, I had taken the job." Connors has been with the company ever since, moving over to their Horizons restaurant as head chef and then, two years ago, helping to plan and launch Aqua Riva. Her kitchen philosophy is simple: "Give people what they want, but do it your own way." She favours food that she calls, "Honest—not pretentious, but well presented."

Chilean Sea Bass with Three Mustards

Sea bass is light and delicate in texture with a delicious flavour. It marries well with the piquant sweetness of the mustards. You can omit the mustard seeds if you like. Sea bass also goes very nicely with savoury relishes or fruit salsas.

Serves 4		Deb Connors
2 Tbsp.	olive oil	30 mL
1/2 cup	diced white onion	120 mL
1 tsp.	minced garlic	5 mL
1 Tbsp.	grainy mustard	15 mL
1 Tbsp.	Dijon mustard	15 mL
1/4 cup	white wine	60 mL
1/2 cup	chicken stock	120 mL
1/2 Tbsp.	cornstarch	7.5 mL
1/2 cup	heavy cream	120 mL
	sea salt and freshly ground black pepper to taste	
4	6-oz. (170-g) sea bass fillets	4
	sea salt and freshly ground black pepper to taste	
2 Tbsp.	toasted yellow mustard seeds	30 mL
3 Tbsp.	olive oil	45 mL

Heat the 2 Tbsp. (30 mL) olive oil in a medium saucepan over medium-high heat. Add the onion and garlic, reduce the heat to medium and sauté for 2–3 minutes. Stir in the mustards. Add the white wine and chicken stock. Cook over high heat until it is reduced by half. Lower the heat to medium. Combine the cornstarch and cream and whisk until smooth. Whisk the mixture into the other ingredients and simmer 4–5 minutes, whisking often. Season with salt and pepper and strain. Keep warm while preparing the fish.

Season the fillets on both sides with salt and pepper. Place the mustard seeds on a small plate. Press the sea bass firmly into the seeds, on one side only. Heat the 3 Tbsp. (45 mL) olive oil in a large pan over medium-high heat. Place the sea bass in the hot oil, seed-coated side down. Reduce the heat to medium and sauté 3–4 minutes per side. To serve, arrange a sea bass fillet in the centre of each plate. Spoon the sauce over the fish.

Chilean Sea Bass with Tomato, Caper & Niçoise Olive Vinaigrette

The vinaigrette in this recipe is so versatile you can serve it with grilled tuna, salmon or chicken. It's a summer staple in my kitchen.

Serves 8		Lesley Stowe
1	head garlic, roasted (see page 7)	1
1/3 cup	balsamic vinegar	80 mL
1/2 cup	extra-virgin olive oil	120 mL
2 Tbsp.	finely chopped flat-leaf parsley	30 mL
1/2 cup	tomatoes, seeded and finely diced	120 mL
1/4 cup	capers	60 mL
1/4 cup	niçoise olives, pitted, cut into quarters	60 mL
	salt and black pepper to taste	
2 Tbsp.	olive oil	30 mL
8	5-oz. (140-g) fillets sea bass, skin on	8

When the garlic is cool, roughly chop the cloves. Whisk the balsamic vinegar and the 1/2 cup (120 mL) olive oil together. Stir in the garlic, parsley, tomatoes, capers and olives. Season with salt and pepper. Set aside.

Heat the 2 Tbsp. (30 mL) olive oil in a heavy, ovenproof skillet over medium-high heat. Sauté the sea bass 1–2 minutes on one side, until golden. Turn the fillets and place the pan in the oven for 5–6 minutes. Serve each piece with 1–2 spoonfuls of the vinaigrette on top.

Whitefish in a Potato Crust

A much fancier version of fish and chips. Try it—you will love the results.

Serves 6		Caren McSherry-Valagao
2 lbs.	fresh fish fillets (snapper, cod, halibut)	900 g
1/3 cup	flour	80 mL
1	large egg	1
1/4 cup	milk	60 mL
4	large russet potatoes, finely grated	4
2 Tbsp.	olive oil	30 mL
4	fresh lemons	4
1 cup	white wine	240 mL
2	large shallots, minced	2
1 cup	unsalted butter	240 mL
1/4 cup	capers	60 mL
3/4 cup	chopped Roma tomatoes	180 mL
1/2	bunch parsley, finely chopped	1/2

Dredge the fish in the flour. Combine the egg and milk. Dip the fish into the mixture, then press the grated potato onto both sides of the fish. Heat the oil in a non-stick frying pan over medium-high heat. Fry the fish on both sides until crisp and brown, about 5 minutes each side.

To make the sauce, cut the lemon in half, squeeze the juice into a saucepan and add the lemon rinds. Add the wine and shallots. Bring to a boil and cook until the mixture is reduced to 1/3 cup (80 mL). Remove the lemon rinds and whisk in the butter, 1 Tbsp. (15 mL) at a time, until the sauce is smooth and thick. Stir in the capers. To serve, ladle a portion of the sauce on a serving plate, sprinkle the chopped tomatoes over, arrange the fish on top and garnish with chopped parsley.

"Corned" Alaskan Black Cod with Warm Red Cabbage & Pear Slaw

I love Alaskan black cod. It's one of the most versatile fish to work with and one of the most delicious to eat. Some of it is smoked for consumption here, but the shame is that most of it is exported. I buy it in stores that cater to the Southeast Asian population. The corned beef–style marinade suits the richness and texture of the fish perfectly. Instead of the slaw, try sauerkraut or a fluffy pile of potatoes mashed with horseradish. Alaskan black cod also goes by the name of sablefish.

Serves 4		Karen Barnaby
1 1/2 tsp.	whole black peppercorns	7.5 mL
1 1/2 tsp.	coriander seeds	7.5 mL
1 1/2 tsp.	yellow mustard seeds	7.5 mL
5	whole cloves	5
3	bay leaves	3
	large pinch cinnamon	
2 tsp.	paprika	10 mL
1 Tbsp.	Worcestershire sauce	15 mL
1 tsp.	liquid smoke	5 mL
5	medium cloves garlic, peeled and coarsely chopped	5
1/2	stalk celery, chopped	1/2
2 tsp.	salt	10 mL
1 tsp.	sugar	5 mL
4	8-oz. (225-g) skinless, centre cut black cod fillets	4
1 lb.	red cabbage, cored and thinly sliced	454 g
3 Tbsp.	balsamic vinegar	45 mL
1/2 tsp.	salt	2.5 mL
1 tsp.	sugar	5 mL

1 Tbsp.	vegetable oil	15 mL
2	cloves garlic, minced	2
1/2 tsp.	caraway seeds	2.5 mL
1/4 cup	finely diced shallots	60 mL
1	firm ripe pear, cored and diced into 1/4-inch (.6-cm) cubes	1
	freshly ground black pepper to taste	

Coarsely crush the peppercorns, coriander and mustard seeds, cloves and bay leaves in a coffee grinder or mortar and pestle. Place in the workbowl of a food processor or blender with the cinnamon, paprika, Worcestershire sauce, liquid smoke, garlic, celery, salt and sugar. Process to a coarse paste. Coat the fish evenly with the mixture. Cover and refrigerate overnight.

Combine the red cabbage, vinegar, salt and sugar. Mix well and let stand while you prepare the rest of the ingredients. Bring a large pot of water to a boil. Add the marinated cod and turn down to a bare simmer. Cook for 10–15 minutes, until the cod flakes easily. It will remain moist-looking on the inside.

While the cod is cooking, heat the vegetable oil in a large frying pan over medium heat. Add the garlic and caraway seeds. Sauté until the garlic starts to turn pale gold. Add the shallots and cook until they start to turn brown. Add the cabbage mixture and cook, stirring frequently, until the cabbage is crisp-tender. Add the pear and cook until heated through. Season with pepper. Place the slaw on heated plates. Remove the cod from the liquid with a slotted spoon and serve on top of the slaw.

Halibut on Wilted Spinach with Pancetta Mignonette

This may seem an odd combination at first glance, but the halibut has a good meaty consistency and takes very well to the bold flavours of pancetta and balsamic vinegar. The buttery spinach lends colour and a silky texture to the dish. I like to serve it with small potatoes that have been simply tossed in olive oil with salt and freshly ground pepper and roasted in a hot oven.

Serves 4		Deb Connors
1/4 cup	melted butter	60 mL
1 Tbsp.	fresh lemon juice	15 mL
4	6-oz. (170-g) halibut fillets, 1 1/2 inches (4 cm) thick	4
	sea salt and freshly ground black pepper to taste	
1 Tbsp.	softened butter	15 mL
2	shallots, diced	2
2 Tbsp.	white wine	30 mL
12 oz.	cleaned spinach leaves	340 g
	sea salt and freshly ground black pepper to taste	
1 recipe	Pancetta Mignonette	1 recipe

Preheat the oven to 450°F (230°C). Combine the melted butter and lemon juice. Place the halibut fillets on a roasting pan and brush with the lemon butter. Season with salt and pepper. Bake for 8–10 minutes, until the halibut is just cooked through but still moist in the centre.

Heat the softened butter in a large sauté pan over medium-high heat. Add the shallots and cook for 1 minute. Add the white wine and spinach. Remove the pan from the heat and stir until the spinach is just wilted. Season with salt and pepper.

Arrange the spinach in the centre of the serving plates. Place a halibut fillet on the spinach. Spoon the warm Pancetta Mignonette over the halibut, including some of the juices, and serve.

Pancetta Mignonette

Makes about 1/2–3/4 cup (120–180 mL)

1 Tbsp.	olive oil	15 mL
4 oz.	pancetta, cut in 1/4-inch (.6-cm) julienne strips	113 g
4	shallots, julienned	4
2 Tbsp.	balsamic vinegar	30 mL
2 tsp.	fresh lemon juice	10 mL
	salt and black pepper to taste	
2 Tbsp.	butter	30 mL
2 tsp.	chopped Italian parsley	10 mL
1 Tbsp.	chopped basil	15 mL

Heat the olive oil over high heat. Add the pancetta and sauté for 3 minutes.
Reduce the heat to medium-high; add the shallots and sauté for 2–3 minutes. Add
the vinegar, lemon juice, salt and pepper. Cook until the liquid is reduced by 1/3.
Add the butter; remove from the heat and stir to melt the butter. Stir in the parsley
and basil. Set aside and keep warm. This may be prepared up to 1 day ahead.
If you make it ahead, omit the butter and chopped herbs and add them after
reheating.

Paella Valenciana

Paella is the most famous dish of Spain. It was invented about 200 years ago when fish, meat and rice were combined for the first time. The fish and vegetables used in this recipe can be changed according to taste and the time of year. I use halibut in the spring and summer, and Chilean sea bass in the winter. Just use whatever you like and have available.

Serves 8		Tamara Kourchenko
4 Tbsp.	olive oil	60 mL
2	chorizo sausages, thinly sliced	2
8	boneless skinless chicken thighs	8
1	red bell pepper, seeded and thinly sliced	1
1	green bell pepper, seeded and thinly sliced	1
1	red onion, chopped	1
12 oz.	salmon fillet, skinless, cut into 8 pieces	340 g
12 oz.	halibut fillet, skinless, cut into 8 pieces	340 g
4 cups	short grain rice, preferably Spanish, although Arborio can be used	950 mL
8–10 cups	unsalted chicken stock	2–2.5 L
	salt and black pepper to taste	
1 tsp.	Spanish saffron	5 mL
16	shrimp, peeled and de-veined	16
16	clams, scrubbed	16
16	mussels, washed and de-bearded	16
1/2 cup	fresh peas, shelled	120 mL
1/2 cup	fava beans, blanched and peeled	120 mL
1/2 cup	green beans, blanched and cut in half	120 mL

Heat the olive oil in a large flat pan with straight sides or, if you are lucky enough to have one, in a large paella pan. Add the chorizo and cook, stirring occasionally, until some of the fat starts melting.

Season the chicken thighs with salt and pepper and add them to the hot pan. When the thighs start to brown, add both peppers and the red onion. Stir so that the vegetables don't burn. When they start to soften stir in the salmon and halibut. Add the rice and mix with the rest of the ingredients.

Pour 8 cups (2 L) of the chicken stock into the pan and season with salt and pepper. Sprinkle the saffron evenly over the stock. Bring to a boil and then simmer for about 10 minutes. Once the liquid is reduced by about 1/3, arrange the shrimp, clams and mussels on the rice and scatter the peas and beans over top. *Do not stir the rice or cover it!*

Let the paella simmer slowly until the clams and mussels open and the rice is cooked. You may need to add a little more stock if it starts to dry out. The cooking time will vary according to the size of the pan you are using. The best way to know when the paella is done is by tasting some of the rice. Adjust the seasoning and serve right from the pan or arrange on a large, deep platter.

Chicken with Honey, Figs & Herbs

Dried Mission figs are a staple in my cupboard. Supermarkets carry them and stores with organic selections carry the unsulphured ones. Marinating and roasting them with the chicken plumps them into a juicy condiment. The combination of the marinade and boning technique creates an oven-grilled bird with a crispy mahogany skin that cooks in half the time.

Serves 3 to 4		Glenys Morgan
1	chicken, preferably free-range, approximately 3 lbs. (1.4 kg)	1
1	head roasted garlic (see page 7), or 5–6 cloves fresh garlic, minced	1
1 Tbsp.	dried herbes de Provence	15 mL
1/4 cup	fruity olive oil	60 mL
1/4 cup	balsamic or red wine vinegar	60 mL
1/2 cup	honey	120 mL
2 cups	white wine	475 mL
2–3	sprigs each fresh thyme and rosemary	2–3
8 oz.	dried Mission figs, about 12–16	225 g
1 tsp.	kosher or pickling salt	5 mL
	freshly ground black pepper to taste	

Prepare the chicken (or ask your butcher to do it). If doing it yourself, place the bird breast side down and cut alongside the backbone to the neck with sharp shears, using the widest point of the tail as a guide to position the scissors.

Once the backbone is removed, give the top of the breast bone a gentle chop with a knife. The bone may be removed completely, but cracking it will allow the bird to be flattened. Skin side up, press down on the centre of the breast and the bird will flatten.

The chicken should marinate for several hours or overnight for best flavour. A resealable plastic bag or shallow dish is excellent for marinating and turning the chicken. Whisk together the fresh or roasted garlic, herbes de Provence, olive oil, vinegar, honey and wine and add the fresh herb sprigs. Place the chicken and figs in the marinade and refrigerate, turning frequently.

To roast, preheat the oven to 400°F (200°C). Choose a pan that will hold the chicken snugly. A 10-inch (25-cm) frying pan is excellent. Place the figs and herb sprigs in the bottom of the pan. Place the chicken on top and pour the marinade over all. Sprinkle with salt and pepper.

Roast for 15 minutes and reduce the heat to 350°F (175°C). After a total of 45 minutes, check for doneness. A simple test is to push a sharp paring knife through the thickest part of the leg and thigh. If the knife slides through like butter and is very hot to the back of the hand, the bird is done. If there is any resistance, the bird is not cooked.

Remove the bird and figs from the pan and keep warm. Discard the herb sprigs. Degrease the sauce if necessary, using a gravy separator. Return the sauce to the pan and boil to reduce and thicken slightly.

Carve the chicken and serve with the figs and sauce.

Pepper-Crusted Roast Chicken

A whole chicken, rolled in cracked black peppercorns and roasted with a whole heap of garlic. This is not an elegant dinner. It's a guest participation event where the roasted garlic must be plucked from the skins at the table. It's well worth it as it results in a tender roasted garlic clove.

Serves 4		Mary Mackay
1	fryer chicken, about 3 lbs. (1.4 kg)	1
2 Tbsp.	whole black peppercorns, crushed	30 mL
1 1/2 tsp.	salt	7.5 mL
2	lemons, cut into 4 wedges each	2
1 Tbsp.	olive oil	15 mL
1 Tbsp.	unsalted butter	15 mL
4	heads garlic, 1/8 inch (.3 cm) sliced off the top	4

Preheat the oven to 450°F (230°C).

Rinse the chicken under cold water and pat dry with paper towel. Fold and tuck the wings behind the back. Combine the crushed peppercorns and salt. Sprinkle a little of the mixture inside the cavity and rub the rest on the outside of the chicken. Stuff the cavity with 2 lemon wedges, reserving the rest. Tie the legs together over the cavity opening.

Heat a large, ovenproof frying pan over high heat. Add the olive oil and unsalted butter to the pan. Add the chicken, breast side down, and brown. Lower the heat to medium-high and brown the chicken on all sides; this should take about 8 minutes. Turn the chicken onto its back. Break the heads of garlic into cloves and add them to the pan.

Place the pan in the oven and lower the temperature to 425°F (220°C). Bake for 60 minutes, basting every 15 minutes. Remove some of the fat. To test for doneness, stick the tip of a knife into the thigh meat: the juices should run clear.

Remove the chicken from the oven and let sit for 5 minutes. Transfer the chicken to a platter and garnish with the roasted garlic and lemon wedges.

Chicken with Forty Cloves of Garlic & a Mickey of Brandy

Dear Uncle Leo: When we last spoke, you reminded me of the Chicken with Forty Cloves of Garlic and a Mickey of Brandy. Wasn't there another one for a chicken baked in a coconut? Anyway, I decided to forge ahead with it. I think there was white wine and some vegetables, but I decided to keep it simple. The results were fantastic—simple, constrained and elegant with just the sweetness of the brandy remaining. I think I'll need a little more direction with the chicken baked in the coconut, though.

Serves 4		Karen Barnaby
1	3-lb. (1.4-kg) chicken	1
1/2 tsp.	salt	2.5 mL
40	cloves extremely fresh garlic, peeled	40
4	strips lemon peel, cut from the lemon with a vegetable peeler	4
1	bay leaf	1
1 1/2 cups	brandy (1 mickey)	360 mL

Preheat the oven to 350°F (175°C). Cut the chicken through the backbone and spread it out flat. Press on the breastbone with the heel of your hand to flatten it further. Sprinkle both sides with the salt and place in a large, tightly lidded, ovenproof frying pan or pot large enough to accommodate the chicken comfortably. Scatter the garlic, lemon peel and bay leaf around the chicken and pour in the brandy. Heat gently to a boil, cover and place in the oven. Cook for 2 hours.

Remove from the oven and place the chicken on a baking sheet. Pour the garlic and brandy mixture into a narrow container. Spoon off and discard the fat when it rises to the top. Transfer to a small pot and keep warm.

Preheat the broiler to high. Broil the chicken close to the heat until the skin turns brown. Either cut the chicken into serving pieces and place on a heated platter or place the whole chicken on the platter and pour the cooking juices and garlic over the chicken. Serve with good crusty bread to mop up the juices and spread the garlic on.

Chef Margaret's Chicken alla Cacciatora

This was one of the first gourmet dishes I learned to cook as a young teenager. I rediscovered how wonderful it can be when my brother shared with me some of his bounty of freshly harvested wild chanterelle mushrooms. I made the best cacciatora ever! This is my version of the classic Italian dish. The name means "hunter's chicken," hence the fall mushrooms. It's great served with buttered noodles.

Serves 4		Margaret Chisholm
2 lbs.	boneless chicken thighs	900 g
	salt and freshly ground black pepper	
1 1/2 Tbsp.	olive oil	22.5 mL
1/4 cup	flour	60 mL
10	cloves garlic, peeled	10
1	small red onion, very finely chopped	1
1	medium carrot, very finely chopped	1
1	stalk celery, very finely chopped	1
1/2 cup	red wine	120 mL
1	bay leaf	1
2 tsp.	fresh thyme leaves	10 mL
1/8 tsp.	cloves	.5 mL
1	14-oz.(398-mL) can Italian plum tomatoes, chopped	1
1 lb.	wild mushrooms (chanterelles, oyster or cremini), sliced	454 g
1 Tbsp.	butter	15 mL
	salt and freshly ground black pepper to taste	

Preheat the oven to 325°F (165°C). Remove and discard the chicken skin. Season the chicken well with salt and pepper. Heat the olive oil in a large frying pan over medium heat. Spread the flour on a plate. Dip the chicken into the flour and shake to remove the excess. When the oil is hot, fry the chicken until it's golden brown. Remove and set aside.

Lower the heat and add the garlic, onion, carrot and celery to the pan. Cook, stirring occasionally, for about 8–10 minutes, or until soft. Add the wine and cook for 1 minute or so. Stir to dissolve the bits stuck to the pan.

Place the chicken in an ovenproof casserole dish. Add the contents of the pan along with the bay leaf, thyme, cloves and tomatoes with their juice. Cover and bake for 1 1/4 to 1 1/2 hours, or until fork tender.

Meanwhile, sauté the mushrooms in the butter over medium heat until tender, about 6–8 minutes. Set aside. Just before serving, add the mushrooms to the chicken. Return the casserole to the oven and simmer for 5 minutes. Season with salt and pepper and serve hot.

"Mad" Fried Chicken

This recipe comes from the first restaurant I worked at, the Bohemian Café in Ottawa. The two Japanese owners had a menu of six items: a burger, a seafood croquette, a salad, a soup, an item I can't remember and the "Mad" Fried Chicken. I wish I knew where the odd name came from, but it never occurred to me to ask. Whole chickens were cut into 16 pieces and marinated for 3 days. The chicken was salty, crispy and sweet. Deep frying is awkward at home, so I have opted to bake, then broil it. Three days of marinating is optimum, but a day is good too.

Serves 4		Karen Barnaby
2 Tbsp.	minced garlic	30 mL
2 Tbsp.	finely grated fresh ginger	30 mL
1/4 tsp.	black pepper	1.2 mL
1/3 cup	soy sauce	80 mL
1/4 cup	white wine	60 mL
1/2 tsp.	salt	2.5 mL
2 tsp.	sugar	10 mL
1 1/2 lbs.	chicken drumsticks	680 g

In a large bowl, mix the garlic, ginger, pepper, soy sauce, white wine, salt and sugar together. Add the chicken pieces and toss well. Cover and refrigerate for 1–3 days.

Preheat the oven to 350°F (175°C). Remove the chicken from the marinade and arrange in a single layer on a foil-lined baking sheet. Bake for 20 minutes. Turn on the broiler and broil the chicken pieces, turning occasionally, until they are crispy and brown.

Chicken Stuffed with Fennel & Italian Sausage

This stuffed and roasted hindquarter of a chicken is comfortingly crispy on the outside and juicy inside. For a family-style whole bird, add an extra cup of bread to the stuffing and fill the cavity. The sauce makes it perfect to serve with polenta, rice or mascarpone mashed potatoes.

Serves 4		Glenys Morgan
2	large fennel bulbs	2
1	small yellow or red onion, finely diced	1
2–3	spicy Italian sausages, about 4 oz. (115 g) each, meat removed from the casings	2–3
1 cup	coarsely chopped dry bread crumbs	240 mL
1/2 tsp.	ground cinnamon	2.5 mL
1/2 tsp.	ground fennel	2.5 mL
	freshly ground black pepper to taste	
4	chicken hindquarters	4
1 Tbsp.	olive oil	15 mL
1	14-oz. can (398-mL) Italian plum tomatoes, drained, seeded and coarsely chopped	1
1/4 cup	sherry or balsamic vinegar	60 mL

Preheat the oven to 400°F (200°C). Trim the fennel bulbs (the leafy tops may be saved for garnish) and cut them in half lengthwise. Remove the tough bottom and core. Finely dice one fennel bulb and thinly slice the other. Combine the diced fennel with the diced onion.

Choose an ovenproof skillet or pan (cast iron is excellent) large enough to hold the chicken in a single layer. Add the meat of one sausage to the pan and cook over medium-high heat. If the sausage is very lean, add 1 Tbsp. (15 mL) olive oil to prevent sticking. Taste for seasonings—different sausages have varying degrees of salt and spiciness.

Add the finely minced fennel and onion to the pan. Cook until softened. If the pan dries, lower the heat and cover the pan, to sweat the vegetables. When cooked, remove from the heat and allow to cool.

In a mixing bowl, break up the remaining sausages and add the bread crumbs, cinnamon, ground fennel and pepper. Mix in the cooked sausage mixture. Mix well to combine and allow to cool.

On the underside of each thigh, make a slit to the joint of the drumstick, exposing the thigh bone. Crack the joint apart. Use a sharp knife to cut the tendons and scrape away the meat from the thigh bone. Remove the bone. Stuff each thigh with the stuffing. Reshape the thigh. Heat the olive oil in the skillet. Brown the skin side of each leg and remove from the pan. Add the sliced fennel to the skillet and sauté until soft. Add the tomatoes and vinegar. Stir to deglaze the pan.

Return the chicken to the pan, placing it on the tomato and fennel. Roast the chicken in the preheated oven until nicely browned and the chicken tests done, about 40 minutes. Remove the legs from the pan and keep warm. If desired, reduce the fennel and tomato to thicken. Garnish with the reserved fresh fennel leaves.

Tuscan-Style Free-Range Chicken

Serves 5 to 6   *Caren McSherry-Valagao*

1	free-range chicken, 3–4 pounds (1.4–1.8 kg)	1
	cracked black pepper and sea salt to taste	
1	large fennel bulb	1
1	14-oz. (398-mL) can water-pack artichokes	1
1	head garlic	1
1	lemon	1
2 cups	pearl onions, peeled	475 mL
1 cup	oil-cured olives (Arnaud)	240 mL
1 cup	cracked green olives (Arnaud)	240 mL
2 Tbsp.	coarsely chopped fresh oregano	30 mL
2 Tbsp.	coarsely chopped fresh thyme	30 mL
1/2 cup	white wine	120 mL

Preheat the oven to 400°F (200°C). Place the chicken on a cutting board and cut the chicken up the back. Open it up. Lay it flat, skin side up, and press to flatten. Rub it with olive oil and sprinkle with cracked black pepper and sea salt. Set aside.

Slice the fennel thinly and place it in a large bowl. Drain the artichokes and cut them into sixths. Add them to the fennel. Separate the cloves of garlic, but do not peel; place them in the bowl. Cut the lemon into 6 wedges, squeeze the juice over the fennel and drop the wedges into the bowl as well.

To peel the pearl onions, cut the ends off and drop them into boiling water for about 15 seconds. Refresh them in cold water, then drain them—the skins will slip right off. Add them to the other ingredients, along with the olives, herbs and wine. Toss all the ingredients to mix. Place the vegetables evenly in a large roasting pan with the prepared chicken on top. Roast uncovered for 1 1/2 hours.

Remove the chicken from the oven. Pierce the inside thigh with a fork; the chicken is cooked through if the juices run clear, or the internal temperature reads 180°F (82°C).

To serve, cut the chicken into pieces and spoon the vegetable garnish around each serving.

Carpetbagger's Meatloaf

*The "Carpetbagger" in this recipe came from Carpetbagger's
Steak, which is a steak stuffed with oysters. Around the turn of
the century, oysters were so cheap and plentiful that they were
used liberally as a seasoning. Drinking establishments would
give away free oysters to entice customers through their doors.
This recipe idea came from my husband, Steven. It's pretty
darned good—especially when served with cocktail sauce.*

Serves 6 to 8		Karen Barnaby
1 cup	milk	240 mL
2 1/2 cups	1/2-inch (1.2-cm) cubes of good white bread, crust removed	600 mL
2 lbs.	lean ground beef	900 g
1 lb.	ground pork	454 g
3/4 cup	finely diced onion	180 mL
4 Tbsp.	finely chopped parsley	60 mL
1/2 tsp.	salt	2.5 mL
1 tsp.	freshly ground black pepper	5 mL
1	8-ounce (225-g) container shucked oysters	1
6 oz.	lean bacon, finely diced	170 g
3	eggs	3
	cocktail sauce	

Preheat the oven to 350°F (175°C).

Heat the milk in a small saucepan until it is quite hot. Add the bread cubes,
mashing them into a paste. Remove from the heat to cool.

In a large bowl, combine the beef, pork, onion, parsley, salt and pepper. Finely
chop the oysters. Add them and any of their liquid to the meat mixture.

Place the bacon, cooled bread mixture and the eggs in the workbowl of a food
processor or blender and pulse until the mixture is well blended. Or you can mix
it with a whisk until it's well combined. Add to the meat and mix well with your
hands. The mixture will be soft. Pack it into a 10- x 5-inch (25- x 12-cm) loaf
pan. Bake for 1 1/2 hours. Let rest for 10 minutes before serving. Serve with the
cocktail sauce on the side.

Duck Breasts with Roasted Peppers, Honey & Balsamic Vinegar

Duck is very easy to work with if it is cut into separate pieces, such as the breasts and the legs. Most butchers will be able to prepare the duck breasts for you if you give them a little notice. Be careful to cook the meat to medium; it cooks quite fast, especially if the pieces are small. The sweet, slightly sour sauce with a smoky undertone imparted by the roasted pepper complements the rich taste of the duck breast. This dish pairs well with the White Bean & Garlic Mousse (page 137) and Warm Savoy Cabbage Sauté with Smoky Bacon (page 144).

Serves 4		Margaret Chisholm
1	small red bell pepper	1
2	whole duck breasts, cut in half	2
1 1/2 cups	veal or chicken stock	360 mL
1 1/2 Tbsp.	balsamic vinegar	22.5 mL
1 Tbsp.	honey	15 mL
	salt and freshly ground black pepper to taste	
1 1/2 Tbsp.	cold unsalted butter	22.5 mL

Roast the red pepper over a low open flame or under the broiler until charred all over and soft. Place the pepper in a plastic bag and let cool. Peel off the blackened skin. Cut in half and remove the seeds. Dice very finely and set aside.

Trim the duck skin to a 1-inch (2.5-cm) strip. Score the top of the skin with a sharp knife to create a diamond pattern. Cook the duck, skin side down, in a frying pan over medium-low heat until the skin is deep golden and somewhat crisp. Pour off the fat as you go. Turn over and sauté 1 minute on the other side. Place the duck skin side up on a baking sheet. Set aside.

Pour off the excess fat from the pan. Add the stock, vinegar and honey to the pan. Boil on high heat for a few minutes, or until reduced to 1/2 cup (120 mL). Add the diced pepper. Season well with salt and plenty of pepper. (You may prepare the duck and sauce up to this point and chill until 10 minutes before serving time.)

Preheat the oven to 350°F (175°C). Bake the duck to medium doneness, approximately 8 minutes (10 minutes if the duck is cold from the refrigerator). Reheat the sauce and swirl in the butter just before serving. Spoon the hot sauce onto individual plates. Cut the duck breast diagonally into slices, arrange over the sauce and serve immediately.

Oven-Roasted Beef Tenderloin with Balsamic & Frizzled Shallots

This is a dish for entertaining. The never-fail sauce that everyone loves can be made in no time, as long as you have good veal stock, which can be purchased from better quality take-out shops and markets. Unfortunately, there is no substitute.

Serves 8 to 10		Lesley Stowe
16	large peeled shallots	16
1 cup	balsamic vinegar	240 mL
4 cups	rich veal stock	950 mL
3 lbs.	beef tenderloin	1.4 kg
	olive oil	
	salt and black pepper to taste	
1 recipe	Frizzled Shallots (recipe follows)	1 recipe

Preheat the oven to 400°F (200°C). Cut the shallots in quarters lengthwise. Place in a small saucepan with the balsamic vinegar and simmer until approximately 1 Tbsp. (15 mL) of liquid is left. Add the stock and bring to a boil. Simmer to reduce the sauce until it coats the back of a spoon. You should have about 2 cups (475 mL) of liquid.

Trim all the fat and sinew from the beef tenderloin. Rub with a touch of olive oil and season with salt and pepper. In a heavy pan on top of the stove or on a medium-hot grill, sear the meat on all sides. Place on a rack in a roasting pan and roast 20–25 minutes. Remove from the oven and let rest at least 5 minutes. Carve into 1/4-inch (.6-cm) slices. To serve, spoon the balsamic shallots over the beef and sprinkle with a few Frizzled Shallots.

Frizzled Shallots

Makes 1/2 cup (120 mL)

3 cups	safflower or grapeseed oil	720 mL
6	large peeled shallots	6
1 cup	flour	240 mL
1 tsp.	salt	5 mL
1/2 tsp.	pepper	2.5 mL

In a heavy, medium saucepan or wok heat the oil until it's almost smoking. Meanwhile, cut the shallots in half lengthwise and slice in 1/8-inch (.3-cm) pieces. Mix the flour, salt and pepper together in a shallow dish or pan. Dredge the shallots in the flour. Shake off any excess flour and cook the shallots in the hot oil until golden, 1–2 minutes. Remove to paper towels to drain.

Pappardelle with Mushroom Sauce, Braised Endive & Italian Sausage

Filling but not heavy, the braised endive adds an interesting counterpoint to this dish. A favourite meal for a rainy day.

Serves 4		Deb Connors
3	heads garlic, roasted (see page 7)	3
4	Belgian endives	4
6 Tbsp.	olive oil	90 mL
2 Tbsp.	balsamic vinegar	30 mL
	salt and freshly ground black pepper to taste	
2	shallots, peeled and sliced	2
3/4 lb.	mixed mushrooms, sliced	340 g
	salt and freshly ground black pepper to taste	
2 tsp.	fresh thyme leaves	10 mL
2 tsp.	thinly sliced fresh basil	10 mL
2 tsp.	chopped Italian parsley	10 mL
1 tsp.	chopped fresh rosemary	5 mL
3 cups	chicken stock, reduced to 1 cup (240 mL)	720 mL
6	Italian sausages	6

1/2 lb.	dried pappardelle pasta	225 g
2	Roma tomatoes, cut into medium dice	2
4 Tbsp.	butter, softened	60 mL
4	sprigs fresh thyme	4

Squeeze the pulp out of the cooled garlic. Trim the endives and slice them in half lengthwise. Whisk together 2 Tbsp. (30 mL) of the olive oil, the balsamic vinegar and 1 Tbsp. (15 mL) of the roasted garlic. Pour this mixture over the endives and season with salt and pepper.

Heat 1 Tbsp. (15 mL) of the olive oil in a sauté pan over medium-high heat. Add the endives, cut side down, and reduce the heat to medium. Cook for 2–3 minutes, until the endives are light brown. Turn and cook 2 minutes more. They should be translucent but still firm at the base. Remove from the heat. Set aside 4 of the endive halves and keep them warm. Cut the remaining endives crosswise in 1/2-inch (1.2-cm) pieces. Set aside.

To make the sauce, heat the remaining 3 Tbsp. (45 mL) olive oil over medium-high heat until it is very hot. Add the shallots and mushrooms, season lightly with salt and pepper and sauté for 2–3 minutes. Stir in 2 Tbsp. (30 mL) of the roasted garlic. Add the thyme leaves, basil, parsley, rosemary and reduced chicken stock and simmer 3–4 minutes. Remove the sauce from the heat until the pasta is cooked.

Grill, broil or pan-sear the sausages until just cooked through. Cut in half on the diagonal, set aside and keep warm.

Bring a large pot of salted water to a boil. Cook the pasta until just tender, 8–10 minutes. Drain.

To finish the sauce, reheat the mushroom sauce, add the diced tomato and chopped endive, and cook for 1 minute. Remove from the heat and stir in the butter with a wooden spoon until the butter has melted and emulsified.

To serve, toss 1/2 to 2/3 of the sauce with the pasta. Place 3 pieces of warm Italian sausage, cut side down, on each of 4 dinner plates. Using tongs, twirl the pasta in the very centre of each plate so the sausage is partially covered. Spoon the reserved sauce on top of the pasta. Tuck a braised endive half and a sprig of thyme into the top of each pasta twirl.

Mary Mackay

*P*ies, pies, pies. My grandmother and I used to make lots of pies. Well, *Nana* made them, actually, but I like to think that they wouldn't have come out the same without my constant supervision and sampling for quality control. Same with the angel food cakes. And the jumbo raisin cookies, the meat loaf, and that coffee cake smothered in caramel and coconut that we called "hot milk cake." So I guess you could say that my childhood—indeed my whole family life—was filled with food.

My first job, at the age of sixteen, was a waitressing gig, but I soon realized that waitressing was not my calling (I nearly came to blows with a customer). The management decided that I might be happier in the kitchen—and they were right. In 1987 I announced to my parents that I was not going to university as they had planned. I was off to study at the Dubrulle Culinary School. After graduation, I was lucky to meet and work with quite a number of talented people in the food industry who inspired me, trained me and let me find out for myself why food was such an important part of my life.

Anne Milne at Café Splash springs to mind right away. She taught me how to break the rules, and to try new pairings of flavours that my classical French training would never have suggested to me. Diedrick Wolsak of the Frog & Peach provided me with just the challenge I needed after graduating from the Dubrulle School by giving me a kitchen of my own to run. Then there was Lawrence Leier, who taught me how to throw a great dinner party. But I have never been happier than where I am now, working with Michael Lansky at Terra Breads.

At Terra Breads, where I have been head baker since it began in 1993 and partner since 1996, I have deepened my passion for bread-making. I have taught bread-making classes at Dubrulle Culinary School and Barbara Jo's Books to Cooks bookstore; in 1998, I hosted a video on artisan bread-making called *Rolling in Dough*.

I hope that my contributions to this book will inspire you to throw your own great dinner parties, to find fun in food, and to cook with passion.

Beef Fillet 'n' Portobello Chips

*Move over fish 'n' chips. This is sautéed beef tenderloin
with a creamy red-wine sauce, topped with fried portobello
mushroom chips.*

Serves 4		Mary Mackay
4 tsp.	finely chopped shallots	20 mL
2 tsp.	minced garlic	10 mL
1/2 cup	red wine	120 mL
1 tsp.	fresh rosemary, finely chopped	5 mL
1/2 tsp.	cracked black pepper	2.5 mL
4	6-oz. (170-g) beef tenderloin steaks	4
	vegetable or peanut oil for frying	
2	large portobello mushrooms, finely sliced	2
	salt to taste	
1 Tbsp.	butter, unsalted	15 mL
1/2 cup	whipping cream	120 mL

Combine the shallots, garlic, wine, rosemary and pepper in a large dish. Add
the beef and turn to coat. Cover and refrigerate for 1 hour.

Fill a large, deep pot with 2 inches (5 cm) of vegetable oil. Attach a deep-
frying thermometer to the pot and heat to 375°F (190°C). Carefully drop 28
mushroom slices into the pot and stir with a metal slotted spoon, so they don't
stick together. Fry for about 2–3 minutes, then remove with a slotted spoon and
drain on paper towels. Season with salt and keep warm in a low oven while the
meat cooks.

Melt the butter in a large, non-stick frying pan over medium-high heat. Setting
aside the marinade, cook the steaks to your liking, 3–4 minutes per side for
medium-rare. Remove from the pan, and keep warm on plates in a low oven.
Place the remaining sliced mushrooms in the pan and sauté for 1 minute. Add
the marinade and cream and cook until the sauce thickens slightly.

To assemble, spoon the sauce over the fillets and pile 7 portobello chips on top
of each steak.

Pork Tenderloin with Spice Rub & Balsamic Currants

I keep a jar of currants soaking in balsamic vinegar in the refrigerator. The longer they marinate the softer and more flavourful they become. Plump the currants by soaking 1/4 cup (60 mL) currants in 1/3 cup (80 mL) balsamic vinegar for at least 1 hour. To speed the process, gently heat on low for 5 minutes and let cool.

Serves 4 to 6		Glenys Morgan
1 tsp.	ground cumin	5 mL
1 tsp.	ground coriander seed	5 mL
1/2 tsp.	ground cinnamon	2.5 mL
	pinch cayenne	
1 1/2 lbs.	pork tenderloin, trimmed	680 g
2 Tbsp.	olive oil	30 mL
	salt and freshly ground black pepper to taste	
1 tsp.	Dijon mustard	5 mL
1/2 cup	balsamic-soaked currants	120 mL
1 cup	chicken stock	240 mL
1 tsp.	fresh thyme leaves	5 mL
2 tsp.	brown sugar or maple syrup (optional)	10 mL

Combine the dry spices. Rub the tenderloin with 1 Tbsp. (15 mL) of the olive oil and coat with the spices. Wrap in plastic wrap. Leave at least 20 minutes for some flavour to develop, or prepare ahead and refrigerate for a more intense flavour. When ready to cook, preheat the oven to 400°F (200°C).

In an ovenproof skillet, heat the remaining olive oil until very hot. Unwrap the tenderloin and sear to create a nicely brown exterior. Season with salt and pepper. Place the tenderloin in the preheated oven for 15 minutes. Remove from the pan and wrap to keep warm.

Drain off any excess fat from the skillet and add the Dijon mustard to the pan, whisking to incorporate any pan juices. Add the currants, chicken stock and thyme. Reduce over medium-high heat to a syrupy consistency. Taste and adjust the seasonings. For a sweeter sauce add the sugar or syrup. When the sauce has thickened, slice the pork and add any juice from the meat to the sauce. Serve drizzled with the sauce and scatter the currants as a garnish.

Mustard & Herb-Crusted Lamb Chops

Rack of lamb is a wonderful main course. Judging the cooking time can be tricky, and cutting the rack when it is hot more so. I have found that cutting the chops prior to cooking and generously rubbing my herb mixture on both sides not only solves the cooking and cutting dilemma, but offers double the crusty rub. The term Frenched simply indicates that the chop has the rib bone cleaned and exposed so that it can be picked up and eaten with your fingers. There are approximately 7 chops per rack; purchase accordingly.

Serves 6		Caren McSherry-Valagao
4	Frenched racks of lamb	4
1/3 cup	Dijon mustard	80 mL
4	cloves garlic, minced	4
3 Tbsp.	extra-virgin olive oil	45 mL
2 Tbsp.	finely chopped fresh thyme	30 mL
2 Tbsp.	finely chopped fresh basil	30 mL
2 Tbsp.	finely chopped fresh rosemary	30 mL
2 Tbsp.	finely chopped fresh sage	30 mL
1 1/2 tsp.	sea salt	7.5 mL
1 Tbsp.	freshly cracked black pepper	15 mL

Trim any visible fat from the rack and carefully cut the chops evenly. If you feel uncomfortable doing this, have your butcher cut them for you.

In a medium bowl, combine the Dijon mustard, garlic and oil. Stir all the herbs into the mustard mixture. Stir in the sea salt and pepper.

Rub the garlic and herb mixture over both sides of the chops. Heat your barbecue or grill to high, and grill each side for about 3–4 minutes (for medium-rare). Turn the meat only once so that it doesn't dry out.

Serve immediately.

Braised Lamb Shanks on Flageolet Beans

Braised dishes are very rewarding and comforting. They take a long time to make, but once they are done, they last for a long time and are very easy to reheat. I like serving them for parties: everything can be ready ahead of time and I can spend the evening with my guests instead of in the kitchen. This lamb is good with mashed potatoes as well as the Flageolet Beans.

Serves 6		Tamara Kourchenko
1/4 cup	vegetable oil	60 mL
6	lamb shanks, about 1 lb. (454 g) each	6
	salt and black pepper to taste	
2	medium white onions, peeled	2
2	stalks celery	2
1	large carrot, peeled	1
4 oz.	pancetta or bacon	113 g
6	plum tomatoes	6
1/4 cup	olive oil	60 mL
3	cloves garlic, chopped	3
3	anchovies, chopped	3
2 cups	dry sherry	475 mL
6 cups	unsalted chicken stock	1.5 L
1	bay leaf	1
1 Tbsp.	chopped fresh thyme	15 mL
1	cinnamon stick, about 4 inches (10 cm) long	1
3	cloves, whole	3
1	orange	1

Preheat the oven to 350°F (175°C). Heat the vegetable oil to smoking hot in a large pan. Season the lamb with salt and pepper and brown on all sides. Do a couple at a time to make sure all the sides are brown. Place the shanks in an ovenproof dish or roasting pan large enough to hold them, preferably in one layer.

Cut the onions, celery, carrots and pancetta in 1/4-inch (.6-cm) dice. Slice the tomatoes in half lengthwise and remove the seeds. Cut into 1/4-inch (.6-cm) dice.

Heat the olive oil in a large pot. Add the onions, celery, carrots, pancetta and garlic. Cook over medium heat, stirring, until the vegetables begin to turn brown. Add the chopped anchovies and tomatoes and cook for 2 minutes longer. Stir in the sherry and cook for about 5 minutes. Add the chicken stock, bay leaf, thyme, cinnamon stick and cloves. Cut the orange in quarters, squeeze the juice into the sauce and then add the pieces. Bring to a boil and pour over the lamb shanks. Cover with foil and place in the oven for about 2 hours or until the meat falls off the bone. Turn the shanks after 1 hour, so they cook evenly.

Remove the shanks from the sauce and keep warm. Strain the sauce and keep the vegetables, but discard the orange pieces, cinnamon stick, bay leaf and cloves (if you can find them). Bring the sauce back to a boil and reduce until it thickens slightly. Pour the vegetables and sauce over the meat.

Flageolet Beans

Serves 6

Flageolet are small, pale green French beans with a low starch content. I like them because of their creamy texture and beautiful colour. If you can't find flageolet, the next best is cannellini beans.

2 cups	flageolet beans, rinsed, picked over and soaked overnight	475 mL
1	clove garlic, peeled	1
2	sprigs fresh thyme	2
1	bay leaf	1
2 Tbsp.	extra-virgin olive oil	30 mL
	salt and black pepper to taste	

Drain the beans and place in a large pot together with all the other ingredients except the salt and pepper. Pour cold water over them until the beans are covered by about 2 inches (5 cm) of liquid. Bring to a boil. Lower the heat and simmer until the beans are very soft, about 2 hours. You may need to add more water if it reduces too fast. Toward the end of the cooking period, season with salt and pepper. Drain the beans and pick out the garlic, thyme and bay leaf.

Moroccan Spiced Braised Lamb, Vegetables & Olives

My travels in Africa forever changed my outlook on spice in my life. This is not a traditional tagine, *but a combination of flavour memories in a dish that's more French in style, with a healthy helping of vegetables included. Serve over couscous or with soft pita or even chapatis.*

Serves 6 to 8		Glenys Morgan
3 Tbsp.	olive oil	45 mL
3 lbs.	boneless lamb shoulder, cut into 2-inch (5-cm) cubes	1.4 kg
	salt and freshly ground black pepper to taste	
6	cloves garlic, minced	6
2	medium onions, chopped into 1-inch (2.5-cm) pieces	2
2	cinnamon sticks	2
1 tsp.	ground ginger	5 mL
1 tsp.	ground coriander	5 mL
1 tsp.	turmeric	5 mL
1 Tbsp.	ground cumin	15 mL
1/2 tsp.	cayenne	2.5 mL
1/2 tsp.	saffron threads	2.5 mL
1	28-oz. (796-mL) can Italian plum tomatoes	1
4 cups	chicken stock	950 mL
2	large thick carrots, peeled and cut into 2-inch (5-cm) pieces	2
2	white turnips, peeled and quartered	2
1	small butternut squash, about 1 lb. (454 g), peeled and cut into 1-inch (2.5-cm) cubes	1
1 tsp.	salt	5 mL
	freshly ground black pepper to taste	
1 cup	large green olives, preferably not pitted	240 mL
1 cup	pitted prunes or Mission figs	240 mL
1 Tbsp.	each butter and flour, mixed together (optional)	15 mL
1	bunch cilantro leaves, minced	1

Preheat the oven to 350°F (175°C). For a one-pot meal, choose a Dutch oven that works for browning the meat, holds all the ingredients for braising and goes to the table. Or choose a good skillet and work in batches, transferring to an ovenproof casserole.

Heat 2 Tbsp. (30 mL) of the olive oil in the pan until very hot. If necessary, work in batches to brown the lamb without crowding. The lamb will not cook through but should have a good brown colour. If the pan seems dry, add more of the oil. Remove the meat from the pan and lightly season with salt and pepper.

Add 1 Tbsp. (15 mL) of the olive oil to the same pan and reduce the heat. Cook the garlic and onion until softened, being careful to not let it burn. Add the cinnamon sticks, ginger, coriander, turmeric, cumin, cayenne and saffron to the onion and stir to bring out the aroma. Add the tomatoes to the pan and raise the heat. Bring the spiced tomato and onion mixture to near boiling, stirring to deglaze the pan.

Return the meat to the pan. Pour in 3 cups (720 mL) of the chicken stock—enough to cover the meat by 1 inch (2.5 cm). Cover and place in the preheated oven. Bake for 1 1/2 hours before adding the carrots, turnips and squash. Stir in the salt and pepper. Add the olives and prunes or figs to the top of the stew.

Cover the pan and return to the oven for 1/2 hour. The tenderness of the lamb determines when the dish is done—it should be meltingly fork tender. Test the vegetables. When done, remove the casserole from the oven. If a thicker sauce is desired, stir in the flour and butter mixture, cooking for several minutes to thicken the juices. Remove the cinnamon sticks. Top with freshly minced cilantro and serve.

*O*rreciette with Braised Lamb & Rapini

Orreciette is the consummate al dente pasta. It takes a little longer to cook, but it is wonderfully sturdy and robust. Substitute penne or rotini if you can't find orreciette. Rapini is Italian broccoli and is something of an acquired taste. If it's not available, substitute broccoli.

Serves 4		*Margaret Chisholm*
1 lb.	boneless lamb shoulder, cut into 1-inch (2.5-cm) cubes	454 g
	salt and black pepper to taste	
2 Tbsp.	olive oil	30 mL
1	medium red onion, finely chopped	1
2 oz.	pancetta, chopped	57 g
2	cloves garlic, finely chopped	2
2 Tbsp.	tomato paste	30 mL
1/2 cup	red wine	120 mL
2 cups	chicken stock or water	475 mL
1/2 tsp.	red pepper flakes	1.2 mL
1	bunch rapini or broccoli, thick stems removed	1
1 lb.	orreciette or rotini pasta	454 g
	freshly grated Romano cheese	

Season the lamb with salt and pepper. Heat the olive oil over medium heat. When the oil is hot, almost smoking, add the lamb cubes and cook until well browned on all sides. Remove the lamb from the pan and set aside.

Lower the heat to medium-low and add the onion, pancetta and garlic. Cook for 8–10 minutes, or until the onions are soft. Add the tomato paste; cook and stir for 2 minutes. Add the wine, stock or water, red pepper flakes and lamb cubes. Simmer on low heat, uncovered, for 1 1/2 hours, or until the lamb is very tender, adding a little water if it gets dry.

Plunge the rapini into a large pot of boiling water for 4 minutes. If you are using broccoli, cook it only 2 minutes. Drain and chill in cold water. Drain and set aside.

Bring a large pot of water to a boil. Add the pasta and a heaping tablespoon (15 mL) of salt to the boiling water. Cook, stirring occasionally, until the pasta is tender but still firm to the bite, 9–11 minutes. Drain and return to the pot.

While the pasta is cooking, add the rapini or broccoli to the lamb and cook over medium heat for about 4 or 5 minutes. Add a little water or stock if necessary to create a thin sauce. Season with salt and pepper. Toss with the cooked pasta. Transfer to a serving bowl and sprinkle with the Romano cheese.

Vegetables

Caramelized Onion & Potato Gratin

This dish evolved when I realized how naturally buttery a Swedish, Yukon Gold or Fraser Valley Gold potato could be. A little crafty cookery turned it into a favourite in my "low fat" classes. Poaching the potatoes brings out the starch, which thickens the skim milk nicely. The roasted garlic and caramelized onions add another layer of rich flavour at no calorie expense.

Serves 4 to 6		Glenys Morgan
2 Tbsp.	butter	30 mL
1	large onion, finely diced or sliced lengthwise into julienne strips	1
2 Tbsp.	flour	30 mL
3 cups	skim milk	720 mL
4–6	medium-large yellow-flesh potatoes, peeled and thinly sliced into rounds	4–6
1	small head garlic, roasted (see page 7)	1
1 tsp.	salt and freshly ground black pepper	5 mL

Preheat the oven to 375°F (190°C). Butter a 2-quart (2-L) gratin or lasagna dish, or use a vegetable spray. Heat the butter in a large skillet over medium-high heat. Add the onion and stir to coat well. After several minutes the onion should release its juices and begin to soften. Reduce the heat to medium-low. Let the onion cook very slowly, developing colour. If the pan appears to be drying out, cover and let the onion sweat. The onion should be juicy and a rich caramel colour.

Stir in the flour, raise the heat and let the flour cook. If a golden paste develops on the bottom of the pan, even better. Stir in the milk. When it is hot, add the potatoes. Poach for 3–4 minutes. The edges of the potato slices will be slightly translucent; do not overcook.

Use a slotted spoon to transfer the potatoes and onions to the baking dish. Remove the roasted garlic from the bulb and whisk the cloves—whole or mashed—into the milk. Season with salt and pepper. Pour over the potatoes. Nestle the empty head of garlic in the centre of the potatoes—root side up—for a French touch. Bake until golden and bubbly on top, about 30–35 minutes.

Crispy Potatoes with Garlic, Ginger & Black Pepper

Home fries, move over! This is one of the most delicious potatoes in the pan-fried category you will ever come across. The lengthy cooking tones down the black pepper, but it still makes its presence known.

Serves 4		Karen Barnaby
1 1/2 lbs.	small new potatoes	680 g
1	3-inch (7.5-cm) piece fresh ginger, peeled	1
4	cloves garlic	4
4 Tbsp.	water	60 mL
3/4 tsp.	salt	4 mL
1 1/2 tsp.	coarsely ground black pepper	7.5 mL
2 Tbsp.	vegetable oil	30 mL
2 Tbsp.	coarsely chopped cilantro	30 mL
2	green onions, thinly sliced	2
	lime wedges	

Scrub the potatoes and place them in a pot. Cover with cold water and cook over high heat until the potatoes are just barely tender, about 15 minutes. Drain and cool completely.

Coarsely chop the ginger and garlic. Place in a blender or food processor with the water and salt. Blend until a fine paste is formed. Add the pepper and pulse briefly to combine.

Cut the potatoes into 1-inch (2.5-cm) cubes.

Heat the oil over medium-high heat in a large, heavy, non-stick frying pan or well-seasoned cast-iron pan. Add the ginger paste and cook, stirring frequently, for about 2 minutes, until the paste separates from the oil. Add the potatoes and cook, turning frequently, until the potatoes are a crusty brown, 7–10 minutes. Regulate the heat to allow the potatoes to become tender and browned without burning. Stir in the cilantro and green onion. Serve garnished with lime wedges to squeeze onto individual servings.

Pommes 7th Arrondissement

*A number of years ago my husband and I ate lunch at a
restaurant in San Francisco called Roti. We both ordered salads
and then we saw plates of golden crispy potato cakes arriving at
most of the tables around us. We couldn't resist. Garlicky,
buttery and crispy—these potatoes were to die for.*

Serves 8		Lesley Stowe
3/4 cup	clarified butter	180 mL
1/4 cup	garlic oil	60 mL
8	medium russet potatoes	8
16	cloves garlic, peeled	16
	salt and black pepper to taste	

Mix the butter and oil together.

Peel the potatoes, cut them in half, and place with 8 cloves of garlic in a pot.
Cover with cold water, bring to a boil and simmer until soft, 20–25 minutes.

Drain the potatoes and cut them into 2-inch (5-cm) chunks. Roughly chop the
boiled garlic. Mince the remaining fresh garlic. Sauté the minced garlic in a
non-stick pan with a little of the butter mixture until soft; remove from the pan.

Pour enough butter mixture into the pan to generously cover the bottom. Press
half the potato chunks and boiled garlic into the pan and season with salt and
pepper. Sprinkle with sautéed garlic, top with the rest of the potatoes and drizzle
with more butter and oil mixture.

Cook on medium-low heat until the bottom is golden. Remove from the heat
and flip onto a plate. Spoon more butter into the pan and slide the potatoes
back into the pan. Continue cooking until golden on the other side,
approximately 20 minutes. Remove from the heat, flip onto a platter and serve
immediately.

Potato Galette

A nice accompaniment to a winter meal.

Serves 6		Deb Connors
6	russet potatoes, peeled	6
1/2 cup	clarified butter	120 mL
	salt and freshly ground black pepper to taste	

Preheat the oven to 400°F (200°C). Line the bottom of a 10-inch (25-cm) springform pan with waxed paper. Brush the paper and insides of the pan with clarified butter.

Using a mandoline or vegetable slicer, slice the potatoes very thinly, about 1/16 inch (.15 cm). Do not rinse the potatoes, as the starch will help hold the galette together. Starting on the outside edge, place the potato slices in concentric circles, overlapping each potato slice, until the bottom layer has been completed. Brush lightly with clarified butter and season with salt and pepper. Start a new layer of potatoes. When it is complete use your hands or the bottom of a smaller springform pan to press the layers firmly together. Brush with clarified butter and season with salt and pepper. Repeat, pressing firmly on each layer, brushing with butter and seasoning until all the potatoes are used.

Place the pan on the middle rack of the oven. Bake for 30 minutes, until the potatoes are cooked through and browned.

Remove from the oven and remove the sides of the springform pan. Place an ovenproof plate on top of the potatoes and flip it over so the galette rests on the plate. Make sure the paper is removed. Place the galette back in the oven until it is nicely browned, about 10 minutes. Cut into wedges and serve.

*Y*ukon Gold Potatoes Mashed with Wheat Berries, Mustard & Cheddar Cheese

I stumbled upon the wheat berry and mashed potato combo while eating a spoonful of wheat berries and checking the mashed potatoes at work a few years ago; I was captivated by the contrasting textures of the chewy wheat and the smooth potatoes. Since then, they have graced rare duck breasts and venison with sour cherry and blue cheese butter. Plain old mashed potatoes and wheat berries are great together, but they become even more of an event when combined with grainy mustard and cheddar. This dish goes well with plainly prepared meats, or have it with a mound of spinach sautéed with prosciutto.

Serves 6		Karen Barnaby
1/2 cup	soft wheat berries, washed and drained	120 mL
1 1/2 lbs.	Yukon Gold potatoes, peeled and cut into 1-inch (2.5-cm) chunks	680 g
2 Tbsp.	unsalted butter	30 mL
1/4 cup	warm milk	60 mL
2 Tbsp.	grainy mustard	30 mL
1 cup	grated, sharp white Cheddar cheese	240 mL
	salt to taste	

Place the wheat berries in a medium saucepan and cover with ample cold water. Bring to a boil, turn down to a simmer and cover. Cook for 1–1 1/2 hours until the wheat berries just start to open, replenishing the water if necessary. Drain, return to the pot and cover. The wheat berries may be prepared several hours ahead up to this point or refrigerated, covered, overnight.

Place the potatoes in a large pot and cover with ample cold water. Bring to a boil, and cook for about 15 minutes, or until tender.

Reserve 1/2 cup (120 mL) of the cooking water and drain the potatoes. Return them to the pot and mash until smooth. Stir in the butter, milk and enough of the cooking water to make the potatoes smooth and creamy. If the wheat berries are cold, warm them in a pot over medium heat with a scant amount of water. Drain them and add to the potatoes. Stir in the mustard and cheese. Check for salt and adjust the seasoning. Serve immediately.

Balsamic Spuds

This salad of roasted potato wedges tossed in balsamic vinaigrette is wonderful hot or cold.

Serves 4		Mary Mackay
1 tsp.	Dijon mustard	5 mL
1 tsp.	honey	5 mL
1/2 tsp.	salt	2.5 mL
1/2 tsp.	finely chopped shallots	2.5 mL
4 Tbsp.	balsamic vinegar	60 mL
1/2 cup	olive oil	120 mL
1 Tbsp.	finely chopped basil	15 mL
	black pepper to taste	
6	medium red potatoes	6
1/2 tsp.	salt	2.5 mL
1 tsp.	olive oil	5 mL

To make the balsamic vinaigrette, whisk together the Dijon mustard, honey, salt, shallots and vinegar. Continue whisking while slowly adding the olive oil. Stir in the fresh basil and pepper. Set aside while preparing the roasted potatoes.

Preheat the oven to 450°F (230°C). Scrub the potatoes, pat them dry and cut each into 6 wedges. Toss the potatoes with the salt and olive oil. Place the wedges in a single layer on a non-stick baking sheet. Bake for 15 minutes, then turn over and bake another 15–20 minutes, until golden brown. Toss with the balsamic vinaigrette before serving.

Fennel Mashed Potatoes

These mashed potatoes are good with any roasted or grilled meats, but the fennel pairs especially well with fish. If you can find Yukon Gold potatoes you will be in for a treat, as they have a buttery flavour and texture.

Serves 6		Margaret Chisholm
2 tsp.	unsalted butter	10 mL
1	small bulb fennel, stalks removed, chopped into 1/2-inch (1.2-cm) pieces	1
5	large russet potatoes	5
2 tsp.	coarse salt	10 mL
2 Tbsp.	unsalted butter	30 mL
3/4 cup	hot milk	180 mL
	salt and freshly ground black pepper to taste	

Melt the 2 tsp. (10 mL) butter in a small frying pan over medium-low heat. Add the fennel and cook, stirring occasionally, until tender, approximately 15 minutes. Set aside.

Peel the potatoes and cut each into 8 pieces. Place in a medium saucepan and cover with cold water and the coarse salt. Bring to a boil and cook over medium heat for approximately 20 minutes, or until the potatoes are tender.

Drain in a colander and return the potatoes to the pot. Place over low heat and toss the pan a few times to dry them out. One or two minutes should be plenty. Put the potatoes through a potato ricer or mash with a potato masher. Return them to the pot. Beat in the 2 Tbsp. (30 mL) butter in small pieces with a wooden spoon. Beat the hot milk in a bit at a time. Stir in the fennel. Season with salt and pepper.

Cumin-Roasted Yams

This dish is a great accompaniment for Pepper-Crusted Roast Chicken (page 96).

Serves 4		Mary Mackay
2	medium yams	2
1 Tbsp.	cumin seeds	15 mL
2 tsp.	olive oil	10 mL
1/2 tsp.	salt	2.5 mL

Preheat the oven to 450°F (230°C).

Scrub the yams under running water, pat them dry and cut into 1/2-inch (1.2-cm) slices. Coarsely crush the cumin seeds in a mortar and pestle or a spice grinder. Combine the cumin seeds, olive oil and salt and toss with the yams.

Place the yam slices in a single layer on a non-stick baking sheet. Bake for 25 minutes, then turn them over and bake another 10–15 minutes on the other side, until golden brown. Place on a platter and serve hot or cold.

Glenys Morgan

There are several anecdotes that could describe my culinary journey. You can take the girl off the farm but…or even that chicken and egg thing. Which comes first, loving food because it's good or good food nurturing what turns into a passion?

Foods of season and region create lasting impressions. My repertoire of tastebud memories just kept growing and it became the guide in my cooking. At eighteen I ate a fire-roasted tomato soup in Spain, bought freshly ground cumin and coriander in the markets in Morocco and cooked my first porcini mushroom in Italy. But I think the greatest lessons came from my family's farm. Eating tomatoes near lengthy rows of basil has set the standard for all future tomatoes. Boxes of pears arrived in August, each pear wrapped in white tissue marked B.C. Tree Fruit. I still remember the perfect sweetness and texture of those pears. Not to mention, I thought it was very considerate to provide paper to wrap the core in when finished. It's easy to understand where food originates when there's Durham wheat growing in the field and cattle in pastures. So I approach each season, like my father the farmer, glad for the change. Different crops and different dishes.

At one time I thought my background in fine arts destined me to become an art teacher. My love of all things culinary altered that course slightly. In 1980 I launched a cooking school at the Culinary Arts Shop in Calgary. Copper pots, French bakeware, Italian pottery and people with a passion for food—I was hooked. Since that day I've opened my own stores and school, consulted on specialty food shops and cookware stores, and for a measure of hard work and great fun, offered two weeks' help to open my friend Diane Clement's new venture, Tomato Cafe. Two years later, the Tomato was a success and I took a breath and began teaching again.

A culinary education helps explain the science of food and demystifies the cooking process. It made me fearless in the kitchen. Working with Jacques Pepin taught me to see that simple food, done to perfection, is just that—simply perfect. Madeleine Kamman and Julia Child encouraged me with their endless knowledge and curiosity, but also their enthusiasm for sharing. My mother honed my tastebuds with some of the finest recipes I have. And now as a teacher at the Dubrulle Culinary School, there's a new crop of enthusiastic cooks tying on aprons,. They want to make and share great food, and I'm still talking about bright red tomatoes and fragrant basil.

Glazed Apples & Chanterelle Mushrooms with Cider Sauce

This is delicious with a crispy roasted chicken or a simple grilled veal chop. I've also layered the warm mixture over arugula and topped it with some chèvre for an inviting warm salad.

Serves 4		Glenys Morgan
1	shallot, finely minced	1
1	sprig fresh thyme	1
1/2 cup	natural cider vinegar	120 mL
2 cups	unfiltered apple cider	475 mL
1 Tbsp.	unsalted butter	15 mL
4	crisp, juicy apples, such as Jonagold or Gala, peeled, cored and thickly sliced	4
6–8 oz.	chanterelle mushrooms, sliced lengthwise and cleaned	170–225 g
	salt and freshly ground black pepper to taste	
1 tsp.	fresh thyme leaves	5 mL
3 Tbsp.	brandy or Calvados	45 mL
6 Tbsp.	chilled unsalted butter, cut into 1-inch (2.5-cm) pieces	90 mL

Combine the shallot, thyme sprig and vinegar. Reduce over medium heat until the vinegar is almost evaporated. Add 1 cup (240 mL) of the apple cider and boil until reduced to a glaze. Add the second cup of cider and reduce by half.

In a skillet, melt the tablespoon (15 mL) of butter. When hot, sear the apples on each side to create a nicely browned look. Add the mushrooms to the pan and cook until softened. Season with salt and pepper, thyme leaves and the brandy. Keep warm while finishing the sauce.

Remove the thyme sprig from the sauce. Whisk in the 6 Tbsp. (90 mL) butter, piece by piece, until incorporated. Adjust the seasonings. Serve the mushrooms with the sauce spooned over top.

Grilled Portobello Mushrooms with Watercress & Pecan Pesto

If you don't have a grill or barbecue you can bake this mushroom dish in the oven. The mushrooms are delicious served with grilled meats or by themselves on a spinach salad.

Serves 6		Tamara Kourchenko
6	portobello mushrooms, about 3 inches (7.5 cm) in diameter	6
6 Tbsp.	olive oil	90 mL
	salt and black pepper to taste	
1/2 cup	basil leaves	120 mL
1 cup	watercress leaves	240 mL
2 oz.	pecans	57 g
1/2 cup	grated Parmesan cheese	120 mL
1/2 cup	extra-virgin olive oil	120 mL
2	cloves garlic, peeled	2
	salt and black pepper to taste	

Rub the mushrooms with the olive oil and sprinkle with salt and pepper. Grill or barbecue on high, skin side down, until you see a bit of juice coming out of the mushrooms. Remove from the grill and let cool.

Combine the basil, watercress, pecans, 2 Tbsp. (30 mL) of the Parmesan cheese, the olive oil and garlic in a food processor and purée until smooth. Season with salt and pepper.

Rub the cavity of each mushroom with some of the pesto and sprinkle each one with 1 Tbsp. (15 mL) of the remaining Parmesan cheese. Reheat on the grill or in a 350°F (175°C) oven until the cheese melts slightly.

Portobello Mushroom Skewers on Wild Greens

Portobello mushrooms are at their best grilled just until they are hot through and steamy. When cooked this way they retain their steak-like texture. Wild greens—a mixture of different lettuces, arugula, radicchio, mustard leaves and baby spinach—are increasingly stocked in grocery stores. If you can't find it premixed, a bed of spinach or red leaf lettuce would do nicely.

Serves 4		Margaret Chisholm
2 oz.	Parmesan cheese	57 g
8	slices pancetta	8
2	large portobello mushroom caps, cut in 1-inch (2.5-cm) cubes	2
8	sage leaves, torn in half	8
2	cloves garlic, finely chopped	2
3 Tbsp.	extra-virgin olive oil	45 mL
	salt and freshly ground black pepper to taste	
4	handfuls mixed wild greens	4
1 recipe	Sherry Shallot Vinaigrette (page 37)	1 recipe

Soak eight 6-inch (15-cm) bamboo skewers in hot water for 30 minutes. Shave the cheese with a vegetable peeler onto a small plate. Wrap with plastic and set aside.

Place the pancetta in a frying pan over medium heat and cook until firm, but not crisp. Remove from the pan and drain on paper towel. Cut each slice into thirds.

Arrange the mushrooms, sage and folded pancetta alternately on the skewers. Fold the pancetta in half before placing it on the skewer. Whisk together the garlic, olive oil, salt and pepper and brush the skewers generously with the mixture. Grill, broil or sauté the skewers for about 3 minutes on each side, or until browned and hot through. Meanwhile, toss the greens with the vinaigrette. Divide the greens among 4 plates. Place the warm skewers on top of the greens. Sprinkle with Parmesan shavings and serve at once.

*B*raised Red Onions
Wrapped in Pancetta

The combination of flavours in this dish is unique: the onions turn sweet, the vinegar gives them just enough tartness and the pancetta adds a hint of saltiness. They are great served with white meats or grilled swordfish or tuna and are also very easy to make.

Serves 6		Tamara Kourchenko
3	red onions, about 8 oz. (225 g) each, skin on	3
3/4 cup	Balsamic Vinaigrette (page 33)	180 mL
1/4 cup	water	60 mL
12	thin slices pancetta or bacon	12

Preheat the oven to 350°F (175°C).

Cut the unpeeled red onions in quarters from head to root. Place the wedges on a pan large enough to hold all the pieces in one layer. Pour the vinaigrette and water over them. Bring to a boil, cover with foil and bake in the oven for about 45 minutes, basting them every 15 minutes with the sauce. Let the onions cool in the liquid. When they are cold enough to handle, remove them from the pan, peel the outer skin off and wrap each wedge with one slice of pancetta. The onions can be prepared up to this point 2 days in advance. Keep refrigerated.

Before serving, place the onions on a baking tray, rub with a little oil and bake at 350°F (175°C) until the pancetta is golden brown and the onions are heated through.

Asparagus Stacks in Blood Orange Sauce

Asparagus and blood oranges are best enjoyed in the spring, but are now found in markets most of the year. Ordinary oranges can be substituted for blood oranges.

Serves 4		Mary Mackay
2	blood oranges	2
1 lb.	asparagus	454 g
3 tsp.	unsalted butter	15 mL
2 tsp.	finely chopped shallots	10 mL
1 tsp.	lemon juice	5 mL
1 tsp.	finely chopped fresh thyme	5 mL
	salt and black pepper to taste	

Remove the peel from 1 blood orange with a vegetable peeler. Blanch the peel in boiling water for 2 minutes to remove any bitterness. Place the peel in a strainer and run it under cold water until cool. Finely chop the peel and set it aside. Juice the blood oranges—there should be about 1/2 cup (120 mL).

Snap the tough ends off the asparagus. Using a vegetable peeler, peel the bottom halves of the spears. Steam the asparagus until crisp-tender.

While the asparagus is steaming, prepare the blood orange sauce. Heat a small pot over medium-high heat. Add 1 tsp. (5 mL) of the unsalted butter to the pan and swirl to coat. Stir in the shallots and cook 30 seconds. Add the blood orange juice and lemon juice and reduce until the sauce is slightly thickened. Remove from the heat and swirl in the remaining 2 tsp. (10 mL) unsalted butter and the fresh thyme. Season with salt and pepper.

To serve, pile the steamed asparagus on a platter, pour the blood orange sauce over top and sprinkle with the chopped peel.

Signs of Spring Penne with Grilled Asparagus & Preserved Lemon

Although asparagus is available almost all year round, I look forward to the first local asparagus in late spring. This dish combines three of my favourite foods: pasta, asparagus and lemon. Preserved lemons are easy to make, but you can substitute the zest of 1 1/2 lemons for the preserved lemon.

Serves 8		Lesley Stowe
1 1/2 lbs.	asparagus spears	680 g
2 cups	freshly grated pecorino cheese	475 mL
	freshly ground black pepper	
4	wedges Preserved Lemons (recipe follows)	4
1 1/2 lbs.	Italian dry penne	680 g
4 Tbsp.	olive oil	60 mL
1 Tbsp.	chopped chives	15 mL
1/3 cup	toasted pine nuts	80 mL

Trim off the ends of the asparagus. Grill on medium-high heat for 1–2 minutes per side, or until grill marks appear and the asparagus has wilted. Do not overcook. Cut into 1-inch (2.5-cm) pieces. Combine the cheese and pepper in a small bowl. Rinse the preserved lemons, remove and discard the flesh and cut the peel into 1/4-inch (.6-cm) julienne strips.

Bring a large pot of water and 1 Tbsp. (15 mL) salt to a boil. Cook the pasta until it is al dente, 6–8 minutes. Two minutes before you drain the pasta, combine the oil and 2/3 cup (160 mL) of the pasta water in a large skillet. Heat to a simmer and add the asparagus and julienned lemon. Drain the pasta and add it to the skillet. Add 1/3 of the cheese-pepper mixture. Toss to combine. Repeat with the remaining cheese mixture in two additions. Garnish with chives and pine nuts.

Preserved Lemons

2	lemons	2
1/3 cup	coarse salt	80 mL
1/2 cup	fresh lemon juice	120 mL
	olive oil	

Scrub the lemons and dry them well. Cut each into 8 wedges. Toss them with the salt and place them in a glass jar with a glass lid or a plastic-coated lid. Pour in the lemon juice. Close the jar tightly and let the lemons ripen at room temperature for 7 days, shaking the jar each day to distribute the salt and juice. To store, add olive oil to cover and refrigerate for up to 6 months.

Spring Asparagus

Simple techniques combined with good products usually produce the most satisfying meals.

Serves 6		Caren McSherry-Valagao
1 lb.	tender young asparagus	454 g
2 Tbsp.	good balsamic vinegar	30 mL
1/4 cup	extra-virgin olive oil	60 mL
	sea salt to taste	
	freshly ground five-pepper blend or black pepper to taste	
	Parmesan cheese curls	

Holding the asparagus with both hands at the root end, carefully snap the ends off. The spears will automatically break between the tender part and the tough woody ends. Place the asparagus in boiling water for not more than 3 minutes, until they are just crisp-tender. Do not overcook. Drain immediately and place them in cold water to stop the cooking process and preserve the colour. Drain, roll up in a cloth towel and chill until serving time.

To serve, divide the asparagus among 6 salad plates. Drizzle with the vinegar and oil, a pinch of sea salt and a grinding of pepper. Garnish with a few Parmesan cheese curls.

Note: To curl Parmesan, drag a cheese planer or vegetable peeler across the flat edge of a wedge of Parmesan. Pull toward you and curls appear.

Grilled Vegetables with Lemon Basil Vinaigrette

Great summer fare, perfect with a barbecue. Serve them on a platter, either hot or at room temperature.

Serves 4 to 6		Deb Connors
1/4 cup	olive oil	60 mL
2 tsp.	fresh lemon juice	10 mL
12	medium asparagus spears, trimmed	12
1	red bell pepper, seeds and membrane removed, cut lengthwise into quarters	1
1	yellow bell pepper, seeds and membrane removed, cut lengthwise into quarters	1
1	small red onion, peeled and cut into 8 wedges	1
1	zucchini, cut on the diagonal into 1/2-inch (1.2-cm) slices	1
2	large portobello mushrooms, cut into quarters	2
8	new potatoes, boiled, cooled and cut into 1/2-inch (1.2-cm) slices	8
	salt and freshly ground black pepper to taste	
1 recipe	Lemon Basil Vinaigrette	1 recipe

Preheat the grill.

Combine the olive oil and lemon juice. Brush the vegetables lightly on both sides with the oil. Season with salt and pepper. Grill the vegetables for 2 minutes on each side, or until grill marks appear.

Place in a large bowl, dress with the vinaigrette and serve.

Lemon Basil Vinaigrette

1	head garlic, roasted (see page 7)	1
1 cup	basil leaves, packed	240 mL
2 tsp.	fresh lemon juice	10 mL
1 Tbsp.	chopped red onion	15 mL
2 tsp.	white wine vinegar	10 mL
1 Tbsp.	honey	15 mL
1/2 cup	olive oil	120 mL
	salt and freshly ground black pepper to taste	

Squeeze the pulp out of the roasted garlic. In a blender, purée 1 Tbsp. (15 mL) of the roasted garlic, the basil leaves, lemon juice, onion, vinegar and honey. With the motor running, slowly add the olive oil and season to taste with salt and pepper.

White Bean & Garlic Mousse

This bean purée is a simple alternative to rice or potatoes. It is delicious with roasted meats or poultry. Be sure to add enough cooking liquid to the mixture to make it luxuriously moist.

Serves 4		Margaret Chisholm
1 1/2 cups	dried white beans	360 mL
4 cups	chicken stock or water	950 mL
6	cloves garlic, peeled	6
1	bay leaf	1
1	sprig rosemary	1
1/4 tsp.	salt	1.2 mL
	freshly ground black pepper to taste	

Rinse the beans with cold water and drain. Place the beans, chicken stock or water, garlic, bay leaf, rosemary and salt in a medium saucepan and bring to a simmer. Cover and cook over low heat until very tender, about 1 1/2–2 hrs. Add stock or water as needed to keep the beans covered with liquid. When they are cooked, drain the beans, reserving the liquid. Remove the bay leaf and rosemary. Purée in a food processor with a little of the reserved stock until it's very smooth. Add enough stock to make a purée that is the consistency of soft mashed potatoes. Season with salt and pepper.

Grilled Fresh Artichokes with Roasted Garlic Aioli

This is a very easy preparation for our thorny-looking friends.
The fresh taste shines through without complicated techniques.

Serves 6		Caren McSherry-Valagao
2 Tbsp.	white vinegar	30 mL
6	large fresh artichokes, preferably with the stem attached	6
3–4 Tbsp.	good olive oil	45–60 mL
	sea salt and freshly ground black pepper to taste	
1 recipe	Roasted Garlic Aioli	1 recipe

Bring a large pot of water to a boil, and add the vinegar. Drop in the artichokes and boil for about 30–40 minutes, or until tender. To check that they are cooked, pull on 1 or 2 of the leaves. If the leaves pull out easily, the artichokes are cooked; if you have to tug, let them boil for another 5 minutes and check again.

Remove the artichokes and drain them on kitchen towels, not paper. When they are cool enough to handle, cut them in half lengthwise, through the stem, keeping it attached.

Carefully remove the fuzzy choke from the centre and scrape the thorny part away. Heat a large cast-iron skillet to medium-hot, and add the oil. Sprinkle the cut side of the artichokes with sea salt and pepper. Place them cut side down in the hot pan. Grill for about 5 minutes or until golden brown.

Serve hot or cold with Roasted Garlic Aioli or any other dipping sauce of your choice.

Roasted Garlic Aioli

Makes 1 generous cup (240 mL)

A fabulous dipping spread for almost anything that you want to bring to life.

2	heads garlic, roasted (see page 7)	2
1 tsp.	dry mustard powder	5 mL
	pinch cayenne	
2	egg yolks	2
1/2	lemon, juice only	1/2
1 cup	olive or peanut oil	240 mL
	sea salt and freshly ground black pepper to taste	

Peel the papery skin from the roasted garlic cloves and place the cloves in a blender or the bowl of a food processor. Add the mustard powder, cayenne, egg yolks and lemon juice and purée, scraping the sides of the bowl down occasionally. With the motor running, slowly add the oil. Adjust the seasonings to suit your taste.

*E*ggplant Braised with Tomatoes, Pancetta & Balsamic Vinegar

The celery in this eggplant dish lightens the flavour. Serve it hot, warm or at room temperature with simply prepared meats, fish and fowl. The eggplant may be grilled if you prefer.

Serves 4 to 6		Karen Barnaby
1 lb.	eggplant, peeled and cut into 1-inch (2.5-cm) slices	454 g
	extra-virgin olive oil	
2 Tbsp.	extra-virgin olive oil	30 mL
3	cloves garlic, minced	3
2 oz.	pancetta, finely diced	57 g
1/2 cup	finely diced celery	120 mL
6	fresh sage leaves	6
4 Tbsp.	balsamic vinegar	60 mL
1	28-oz. (796-mL) can plum tomatoes, well drained and coarsely chopped	1
2 Tbsp.	tomato paste	30 mL
	salt and black pepper to taste	
2 Tbsp.	coarsely chopped parsley	30 mL
1	clove garlic, minced	1

Preheat the broiler to high. Lightly brush both sides of the eggplant with olive oil and place in a single layer on a baking sheet. Broil, turning once until golden brown and tender. Cool.

Heat the 2 Tbsp. (30 mL) olive oil over medium heat in a large pan. Add the 3 cloves garlic, pancetta, celery and sage to the pan. Sauté until the celery becomes translucent. Add the vinegar. When it has almost evaporated, add the tomatoes and tomato paste. Bring to a simmer and season with salt and pepper. Cook over low heat for a few minutes until the sauce thickens slightly.

Cut the eggplant slices into 1-inch (2.5-cm) cubes. Add to the sauce and simmer for a few minutes to heat it through. Add the parsley and garlic, mix well and serve.

*J*apanese Eggplant Sandwiches

This is a fantastic way to serve eggplant, full of taste, easy to prepare and good hot or cold. Panko, the Japanese word and style for bread crumbs, gives the crisp, crunchy texture on the outside. It is available in Japanese food stores or any fish market.

Serves 8		Caren McSherry-Valagao
2	leeks (white part only)	2
2 Tbsp.	olive oil	30 mL
1	head garlic, roasted (see page 7)	1
9 oz.	soft goat cheese	255 g
1/2 tsp.	freshly ground black pepper	2.5 mL
4	medium Japanese eggplants	4
2	eggs, lightly beaten	2
2 cups	Panko (Japanese-style bread crumbs)	475 mL
2 Tbsp.	olive oil	30 mL

Slice the leeks in half lengthwise and rinse well under cold water. Thinly slice the leeks across and pan-fry them in the oil until they are crispy and browned. Drain on paper towel and set aside.

Peel the papery skin from the garlic cloves. Combine the roasted garlic, goat cheese, pepper and leeks.

Slice the eggplant into 1/4-inch (.6-cm) slices. Spread some of the cheese mixture onto one slice and place another slice on top to make a sandwich. Dip it into the beaten eggs, letting the excess drip off. Dredge the sandwich in the panko, pressing to ensure that it adheres. Heat a frying pan to medium, add 1 tsp. (5 mL) of olive oil for each batch and pan-fry the eggplant sandwiches until golden brown, about 2 minutes on each side. Serve hot or at room temperature.

Baked Roma Tomato Gratin

I like Roma tomatoes for this simple, do-ahead dish because they are small and meaty. You can serve them hot or let them cool to room temperature and slice them with a serrated knife.

Serves 4		Deb Connors
4	medium Roma tomatoes	4
1 Tbsp.	olive oil	15 mL
2	shallots, peeled and finely chopped	2
1	clove garlic, minced	1
2 oz.	field mushrooms, finely diced	57 g
1	small zucchini, finely diced, approximately 1/2 cup (120 mL)	1
1/2	yellow bell pepper, seeds and membrane removed, finely diced	1/2
2 tsp.	fresh thyme leaves	10 mL
	freshly ground black pepper to taste	
2 Tbsp.	white wine	30 mL
3 oz.	Asiago cheese	85 g
3 Tbsp.	bread crumbs	45 mL

Preheat the oven to 375°F (190°). Slice 1/2 inch (1.2 cm) off the top and bottom of each tomato. Using a teaspoon or melon baller, remove most of the seeds and pulp from each tomato to form a small hollow cup.

Heat the olive oil in a sauté pan over medium-high heat and add the shallots and garlic. Cook for 1 minute, stirring lightly. Add the mushrooms and cook 1–2 minutes. Add the zucchini, yellow pepper and thyme and cook 2 minutes. Season with pepper. Add the white wine and cook 1 minute. Remove from the heat and stir in the cheese and bread crumbs.

Fill the tomatoes with the mixture. Place in a lightly oiled, shallow baking dish and bake uncovered for 10 minutes. Serve immediately.

Skillet-Braised Caramelized Fennel

A great introduction to an under-appreciated vegetable in North America. Sweet, soft and caramelized, this fennel should melt in your mouth.

Serves 8		Lesley Stowe
4	medium bulbs fennel	4
3 Tbsp.	unsalted butter	45 mL
2 tsp.	sugar	10 mL
1/2 cup	fresh orange juice	120 mL
2 cups	water	475 mL
	salt and freshly ground black pepper	
	flat-leaf parsley	

Trim the tops of the fennel bulbs and cut in half lengthwise. Melt the butter in a large skillet over medium heat. Add the sugar and stir until melted. Cook the fennel cut side down until well browned, about 5–10 minutes. Turn the bulbs over and add the orange juice, water, salt and pepper. Bring to a simmer and reduce the heat to low.

Cover the pan and cook until the fennel is soft and most of the liquid has been absorbed, about 20–30 minutes. If the pan becomes dry during cooking, add a little more water. If any liquid is left at the end of the cooking time, increase the heat to medium and continue to cook uncovered until the liquid evaporates. Serve warm, garnished with parsley leaves.

Warm Savoy Cabbage Sauté with Smoky Bacon

This warm cabbage dish is delicious served with any roasted meat, poultry or even sautéed fish. It is easy to do ahead and makes a great addition to an everyday meal or a festive holiday meal. Savoy cabbage is the more wrinkled variety and has a mellow flavour.

Serves 4		Margaret Chisholm
4	slices bacon, finely diced	4
1/4 tsp.	caraway seeds (optional)	1.2 mL
1	clove garlic, finely chopped	1
1	medium zucchini, cut in 1/4-inch (.6-cm) dice	1
1	medium carrot, cut in 1/4-inch (.6-cm) dice	1
1	red pepper, seeded and cut in 1/4-inch (.6-cm) dice	1
3 cups	very thinly sliced cabbage	720 mL
	salt and freshly ground black pepper to taste	

In a large frying pan, cook the bacon over low heat until it begins to brown and is slightly crisp. Add the caraway seeds and garlic; cook and stir for 1 minute.

Add the zucchini, carrot, red pepper and cabbage. Cook and stir for 7–8 minutes over medium-high heat until the vegetables are tender, but still slightly crisp. Season well with salt and pepper.

Asian Greens Tuscan Style

Gai lan appears everywhere when its Italian cousin, rapini, is often hard to find. With all the same great qualities, its peppery nature is tamed by this warm dressing. Never dull, it stands up to spicy grilled sausages or brightens a plate of cold roast chicken. Drizzle any leftovers with a good vinegar and enjoy. This recipe works equally well with asparagus, spinach or watercress, and the warm dressing may be used on a mix of baby field greens with shaved Parmesan as an accent.

Serves 4		Glenys Morgan
1	large bunch gai lan or rapini, about 1 lb. (454 g)	1
6	anchovy fillets, minced	6
4	cloves garlic, minced	4
1 Tbsp.	unsalted butter	15 mL
6 Tbsp.	olive oil	90 mL

Bring a pot of water fitted with a vegetable steamer to a boil. Trim the stem ends of the gai lan and discard any tired leaves. Leave the florets intact.

While the water is heating, combine the anchovy fillets, garlic, butter and olive oil in a small saucepan or skillet. Heat over medium-low heat, whisking to dissolve the anchovy and cook the garlic. Be careful not to burn it. The oil will foam and turn a clear golden colour.

Add the gai lan to the steamer, cover and steam for 2–3 minutes. The stems should be crisp-tender, like thin asparagus. Remove from the steamer and shake off any excess moisture. You can leave it whole or coarsely chop it. The dressing may be tossed with the greens or drizzled over top, making sure the crispy anchovies and garlic are evenly distributed.

Punjabi-Style French Lentils

I love using French lentils. They hold their shape when cooked, which makes them great for salads, and they have a bright yet earthy flavour. Although originally from Le Puy, France, a lot of them are now grown in Saskatchewan. Some natural and gourmet food stores carry them, but they are not necessary to make the recipe. This is a no-fuss method of cooking beans and lentils. I check them every hour or so if I want firm shapely beans, or if texture and appearance are not much of an issue, I'll cook them overnight. This recipe is very simple to prepare, yet packed with flavour. The lentils are fairly spicy, so adjust the cayenne to your taste.

Serves 4		Karen Barnaby
1 1/3 cups	French lentils	320 mL
1 Tbsp.	grated fresh ginger	15 mL
1 Tbsp.	minced garlic	15 mL
2	medium tomatoes, finely chopped	2
1 1/2 tsp.	cayenne	7.5 mL
	salt to taste	
1 1/2 tsp.	Punjabi-Style Garam Masala (recipe follows)	7.5 mL
1	tomato, finely chopped	1
2 Tbsp.	coarsely chopped cilantro	30 mL
2 Tbsp.	finely chopped red onion	30 mL
1 Tbsp.	freshly squeezed lime juice	15 mL
	salt to taste	

Preheat the oven to 250°F (120°C). Pick over the lentils for stones and wash them. Place them in a large pot with 8 cups (2 L) water. Bring to a boil and skim off any foam that rises to the top. Cover with a tight-fitting lid and place in the oven. Check the lentils after 2 hours, or 1 hour for French lentils. They should be tender.

Remove from the oven and mash half the lentils to a paste. Stir in the ginger, garlic, 2 chopped tomatoes, cayenne, salt and garam masala. Cover, return to the oven and cook for 30 minutes longer.

Before serving, combine the tomato, cilantro, onion, lime juice and salt. Serve on the side with the lentils.

Punjabi-Style Garam Masala

Makes 3/4 cup (180 mL)

It is gratifying and rewarding to make your own spice blends. You will rarely find the same sparkle and flavour in a store-bought blend—especially if it has been sitting on the shelf for a while.

3 Tbsp.	coriander seeds	45 mL
3 Tbsp.	cumin seeds	45 mL
2 1/2 Tbsp.	black peppercorns	37.5 mL
2 1/2 Tbsp.	black cardamom seeds (seeds removed from pods)	37.5 mL
1 1/2 tsp.	green cardamom seeds (seeds removed from pods)	7.5 mL
1	2-inch (5-cm) stick cinnamon	1
5	whole cloves	5
1/6	of a whole nutmeg	1/6

Heat a small frying pan over medium heat, add the coriander and cumin and dry-roast, stirring frequently, until the seeds turn one shade darker. Pour into a bowl to cool. Combine with the remaining spices and grind to a powder in a coffee grinder. Store, tightly covered, in a cool dark place.

Roasted Root Vegetables with Rosemary

This wintertime recipe is great with any kind of roasted or grilled meat. It goes amazingly well with the Oven-Roasted Beef Tenderloin (page 105). You can mix and match any of the vegetables as long as you always include either the garlic or the onion.

Serves 8		Lesley Stowe
4 lbs.	fresh assorted root vegetables (see below)	1.8 kg
5–6 Tbsp.	extra-virgin olive oil	75–90 mL
1 tsp.	sea salt	5 mL
1/2 tsp.	freshly ground black pepper	2.5 mL
1	8-inch (20-cm) sprig fresh rosemary, chopped	1

Preheat the oven to 400°F (200°C). Toss the prepared vegetables in a bowl with the olive oil, salt, pepper and rosemary. Spread the vegetables on a baking sheet in a single layer. Roast in the upper third of the oven for approximately 20 minutes, or until tender when pierced with the tip of a knife. (Put potatoes and sweet potatoes in the oven 10 minutes before the other vegetables as they take longer to cook.) Remove the baking sheet from the oven and transfer the vegetables to a serving platter.

Vegetables to use:

- parsnips, peeled and sliced on an angle into 1-inch (2.5-cm) pieces
- carrots, peeled and sliced on an angle into 1-inch (2.5-cm) pieces
- turnips, white and rutabaga, peeled and cut into 1-inch (2.5-cm) wedges
- red onion, sliced in 1-inch (2.5-cm) wedges
- garlic, whole cloves
- baby red-skinned potatoes, cut in half
- sweet potatoes, cut into 1-inch (2.5-cm) wedges

Desserts

Parfait Mon Cherry

Cherry compote layered with yogurt cheese, topped with caramelized pecans. The leftovers are great with granola for breakfast.

Serves 4		Mary Mackay
3 cups	plain yogurt	720 mL
2 Tbsp.	honey	30 mL
1 lb.	pitted sour cherries	454 g
1/2 cup	orange juice	120 mL
3 Tbsp.	sugar	45 mL
1/8 tsp.	ground ginger	.5 mL
2 Tbsp.	sugar	30 mL
1/2 cup	pecan pieces	120 g

Prepare the yogurt cheese by lining a sieve with cheesecloth or unbleached coffee filters. Mix together the yogurt and honey. Set the lined sieve over a bowl and pour the yogurt into it. Cover the bowl with plastic, refrigerate and allow to drain for 24 hours.

In a medium pot stir together the sour cherries, orange juice, 3 Tbsp. (45 mL) sugar and ground ginger. Bring to a boil over medium-high heat. Reduce the heat to low and cook, stirring every 5 minutes, until slightly thickened, about 30 minutes. Remove from the heat and cool. The cherry compote can be made a day ahead and stored in the refrigerator.

Prepare the caramelized pecans on the day you plan to serve the parfait. Place the 2 Tbsp. (30 mL) sugar in a small non-stick frying pan over medium-high heat. Stir with a wooden spoon until the sugar liquifies. Add the pecan pieces and stir to coat. Cook until the sugar turns a golden brown colour. Remove from the heat and spread onto a baking sheet to cool. When it is cool, break it into small pieces.

To assemble the parfaits, remove the yogurt cheese from the sieve, discarding the cheesecloth and the drained liquid. Stir the yogurt cheese until smooth; you should have about 2 cups (475 mL). Layer the cherry compote and yogurt cheese in 4 champagne glasses, making several layers of each, and top each glass with caramelized pecans.

Pannacotta with Basil & Cracked Black Pepper Strawberries

Pannacotta is one of my favourite Italian desserts. Light, smooth, easy to make—a perfect summer dessert. If you are pressed for time, serve the Basil and Cracked Black Pepper Strawberries on their own or with ice cream.

Serves 8		Lesley Stowe
2 1/2 tsp.	gelatin	12.5 mL
5 1/3 Tbsp.	water	80 mL
3 cups	heavy cream	720 mL
2/3 cup	icing sugar	160 mL
1/2	vanilla bean, slit lengthwise	1/2
1 recipe	Basil & Cracked Black Pepper Strawberries	1 recipe

In a small bowl soften the gelatin in the water; set aside. Combine the cream, icing sugar and vanilla bean in a saucepan. Bring to a boil. Remove from the heat, remove the vanilla bean and add the gelatin. Gently stir to dissolve. If all the gelatin does not dissolve, heat gently and stir until it does.

Pour the mixture into 8 ramekins. Chill for a minimum of 2 hours. To unmold, run a hot knife around the inside of each ramekin and turn onto individual plates. Garnish with Basil and Cracked Black Pepper Strawberries.

Basil & Cracked Black Pepper Strawberries

Makes about 1 1/2 cups (360 mL)		
1 lb.	fresh strawberries	454 g
1/3 cup	orange muscat dessert wine	80 mL
1/2 tsp.	freshly cracked black pepper	2.5 mL
6	large basil leaves	6

Cut the strawberries into quarters. Toss with the wine and black pepper. Just before serving, shred the basil and stir it in.

Caren McSherry-Valagao

I began my career in the early seventies as a flight attendant for what was then Canada's largest international airline. Weekly trips to the food capitals of the world were a major influence on my culinary career. My interest in food was piqued, and the opportunity to explore the fabulous markets of Thailand, Japan, France, Italy and Portugal offered a tremendous opportunity to pursue the culinary cultural differences of these areas. Working with chefs from around the world taught me the authentic usage of indigenous spices and preparations of local produce and seafood. From this basic understanding, I could then create and modify recipes using ingredients readily available in Canadian markets—remember this was late seventies. What we now consider basics were exotic back then!

My professional training was at the Culinary Institute of America, Cordon Bleu in London, England, and the Thai Cooking School in Bangkok, to name a few. In 1978 I founded Caren's Cooking School. I began with classes of six people sitting in my home kitchen—now we are western Canada's longest-running, privately owned school.

In addition to teaching, I am the garden chef on CBC-TV's *Canadian Gardener* show with host David Tarrant. I am also a Saturday Morning Chef on BCTV'S Saturday morning news, and host Vancouver's first Food and Wine Show, on radio station CKNW.

In 1997, Crystal Cruise Lines invited me to cook aboard their ship *Crystal Harmony* on an Eastern Mediterranean voyage. I created dishes indigenous to each country we visited.

In 1994, I wrote and published my first cookbook, *Vancouver Cooks with Caren McSherry*.

My professional life seems to balance itself with family—my daughter, Christina, son Jason, and husband Jose, who equally shares my passion for fine food and wine.

Chocolate Pâté

The most divine, decadent, comforting, satisfying dessert to pass your lips in decades. The Dutch-process cocoa powder is necessary to give this pâté its deep and dark colour. It is available in European delis and specialty stores. Jump in, make it and reap the accolades.

Serves 15 to 20		Caren McSherry-Valagao
1/2 cup	toasted chopped pistachio nuts	120 mL
1/2 cup	toasted chopped almonds	120 mL
1/3 cup	sun-dried cranberries	80 mL
1/3 cup	sun-dried blueberries	80 mL
1 cup	chopped amaretti cookies, heaping	240 mL
1 tsp.	orange zest	5 mL
1 tsp.	lemon zest	5 mL
3/4 cup	chopped semisweet chocolate	180 mL
5 Tbsp.	brandy, rum or other liquor	75 mL
1/2 cup	sugar	120 mL
1	egg	1
2	egg yolks	2
3/4 cup	unsalted butter, at room temperature	180 g
1 cup	dark Dutch-process cocoa powder	240 mL

Line a 3- x 9-inch (7.5- x 23-cm) loaf pan, or equivalent, with plastic wrap. Mix the nuts, fruits, cookies and both zests together in a large bowl. Set aside.

Melt the chocolate over a double boiler. In a small pot, heat the liquor and sugar together, stirring until the sugar dissolves. Beat the egg and yolks together and whisk into the sugar mixture. In a large mixing bowl, beat the butter until creamy. Add the cocoa powder, egg mixture and melted chocolate. The mixture will be thick and creamy. Pour this over the nut and fruit mixture and stir well to combine. Turn the mixture into the prepared pan, pressing down so there are no air bubbles. Chill for at least 4 hours or overnight.

To serve, invert the mold onto a serving dish, peel off the plastic wrap, slice into thin pieces and garnish with fresh berries if available. *Note:* This dessert can be frozen for up to 2 weeks.

Frozen Mocha Terrine with Warm Framboise Sauce Anglaise

This is a great dessert to make ahead, since it lasts very well in the freezer. You can change the flavour of the sauce by adding different liqueurs, or garnish the terrine with fresh berries. Either way, the results are sinful.

Makes 1 terrine		Tamara Kourchenko
1 1/2 cups	unsalted butter, softened	360 mL
1 1/3 cups	cocoa powder	320 mL
1 Tbsp.	finely ground espresso beans	15 mL
3 Tbsp.	coffee liqueur	45 mL
7	large egg yolks at room temperature	7
3/4 cup	sugar	180 mL
1/4 cup	water	60 mL
5 oz.	semisweet chocolate, chopped	140 g
2 cups	whipping cream	475 mL
1/4 cup	sugar	60 mL
1 recipe	Framboise Sauce Anglaise	1 recipe

In the bowl of an electric mixer, with the paddle attachment, beat the butter until light and fluffy. Add the cocoa, espresso and coffee liqueur and keep on beating until everything is incorporated and the mixture is creamy, about 7 minutes. Transfer the mixture to another bowl.

Clean the mixer bowl and, with the whisk attachment, whip the egg yolks until light in colour, creamy and tripled in volume. Combine the 3/4 cup (180 mL) sugar and water in a small pot. Bring to a boil and cook, without stirring, for about 6 minutes or until a candy thermometer reaches 240°F (115°C). Whisk the sugar syrup in a slow steady stream into the egg yolks. Keep whisking at medium-high speed while you melt the chocolate in a double boiler. Add the chocolate to the egg mixture. Keep whisking until the mixture is cold, about 8 minutes. With a spatula, fold the egg mixture into the butter mixture.

Clean the mixer bowl again and use it to whisk the cream until soft peaks form. Add the 1/4 cup (60 mL) sugar and continue beating until stiff peaks form. Fold 1/3 of the cream into the chocolate mix to lighten it. Carefully, but thoroughly, fold in the remaining cream in 2 additions. Pour the mixture into an 8-cup (2-L) terrine mold or loaf pan. Cover with plastic and freeze overnight.

To unmold, dip the pan briefly in hot water and invert onto a platter. Slice and serve over the warm sauce.

Framboise Sauce Anglaise

Makes 2 1/2 cups (600 mL)

This sauce is delicious warm or cold.

6	egg yolks	6
1/2 cup	sugar	120 mL
2 cups	whipping cream	475 mL
1	vanilla bean	1
3 Tbsp.	raspberry liqueur, such as Chambord	45 mL

Whisk together the egg yolks and sugar. Place the cream in a pot. Cut the vanilla bean in half lengthwise, scrape the seeds into the cream and add the pod. Heat almost to boiling. Add the hot cream to the sugar mixture in a slow, steady stream, whisking constantly. Return the sauce to the pot and cook over low heat, stirring constantly, until the sauce thickens enough to coat the back of a spoon. Strain and cool. Stir in the liqueur.

To serve, heat the sauce until barely warm, or serve cold if you prefer.

Rustic Apple Tart with Balsamic Nectar

The charm of this tart's rustic presentation appeals to any novice baker and the balsamic nectar to the sophisticated dessert lover. Bake on a pizza stone for pastry that's a little crispy. Simply reducing any ordinary balsamic turns it into a syrup that's great on salads or grilled salmon as well.

Serves 6 to 8		Glenys Morgan
2 cups	balsamic vinegar	475 mL
4–5	Golden Delicious apples	4–5
1/4 cup	butter	60 mL
1/2 cup	sugar	120 mL
1	large lemon	1
1 tsp.	vanilla	5 mL
2 cups	flour	475 mL
4 Tbsp.	sugar	60 mL
1/4 tsp.	salt	1.2 mL
3/4 cup	butter	180 mL
1–2 Tbsp.	water	15–30 mL
1	egg yolk	1

Pour the vinegar into a non-reactive saucepan. Heat on the lowest setting possible. Let the vinegar evaporate and gradually reduce. This step may take an hour, and there should be no visible signs of heating. Remove from the heat when the consistency is like maple syrup. Store the balsamic nectar in the refrigerator in a clean glass jar.

Preheat the oven to 425°F (220°C). Peel, core and slice the apples. Melt the butter and 1/2 cup (120 mL) sugar together in a skillet and add the apples. Sauté the apples until softened and coated. Grate the zest from the lemon and add it to the apples. Juice the lemon and reserve 2 Tbsp. (30 mL) for the crust. Remove the apples from the heat and stir in the remaining lemon juice and vanilla. Allow the filling to cool while making the crust.

Combine the flour, sugar and salt. Cut the butter into small cubes and distribute over the flour. Work the butter into the flour, using a pastry blender or your fingertips, until the butter resembles large oatmeal flakes in the flour. Mix the 2 Tbsp. (30 mL) lemon juice with the water and egg yolk. Add the liquid to the flour and butter mixture and blend, shaping the dough into a ragged ball.

Lightly flour the rolling surface and flatten the ball of dough. Roll into a 12- to 14-inch (30- to 35-cm) round. The edges will be irregular. Slide the dough onto a large cookie sheet or pizza stone. If the cookie sheet has sides, turn it over and use the bottom.

Centre the apples and spread out to within 2 inches (5 cm) of the edge. The apples should be gently mounded in the centre and slightly thinner towards the edge. Loosely fold the edges of the dough back over the apples.

Bake for 10 minutes, then reduce the heat to 375°F (190°C). Cook until the pastry is golden. Cool the pie until just warm before serving. Cut into wedges and drizzle some of the balsamic nectar over the apple filling.

Chocolate Chip Meringues with Grand Marnier Whipped Cream & Strawberries

Make meringues whenever you have extra egg whites. They are very easy to make and last for about 2 weeks in an airtight container. If you don't need a whole dessert, but have the egg whites handy, you can always make this and serve it like a cookie with coffee.

Serves 6		Tamara Kourchenko
3	egg whites	3
1/8 tsp.	salt	.5 mL
1 tsp.	fresh lemon juice	5 mL
1 cup	sugar	240 mL
1/2 cup	semisweet chocolate, coarsely chopped	120 mL
1 cup	heavy cream	240 mL
2 Tbsp.	sugar	30 mL
1 Tbsp.	Grand Marnier	15 mL
1 lb.	strawberries, cut into quarters	454 g
1 Tbsp.	sugar	15 mL
2 Tbsp.	Grand Marnier	30 mL

Preheat the oven to 225°F (105°C). Line two baking trays with foil.

Whisk the egg whites with the salt and lemon juice until they form soft peaks. Gradually add the 1 cup (240 mL) sugar and continue whisking, at high speed, until the mixture is shiny, the sugar is dissolved and stiff peaks form, about 5 minutes. Fold the chocolate into the meringue mixture.

Spread half the meringue into six 3 1/2-inch (9-cm) squares. Use the rest of the mix to make little mounds with a teaspoon to serve as cookies. Bake for 2 hours. Turn the oven off and leave the trays in it for another hour to allow the meringues to dry completely.

Just before serving, whip the cream with the 2 Tbsp. (30 mL) sugar and 1 Tbsp. (15 mL) Grand Marnier until soft peaks form. Mix the strawberries with the remaining sugar and liqueur.

To serve, place one meringue square on each plate. Divide the whipped cream among the meringues and top with the strawberries. Use some of the little meringue cookies for decoration.

Mini Almond Ice Cream Tartuffi

A sensational mini dessert for those who only want to whet their sweet tooth. Others may feel it necessary to drown them with two.

Serves 6		Caren McSherry-Valagao
2 cups	good-quality vanilla ice cream	475 mL
1 cup	chopped amaretti biscuits	240 mL
1/2 cup	bottled brandied cherries	120 mL
1 cup	toasted chopped almonds	240 mL

Soften the ice cream slightly, just so that you can push it into the muffin cups.

Fill the bottom half of a 6-cup (1.5-L) non-stick muffin pan with the soft ice cream. Top each muffin cup with 2 Tbsp. (30 mL) of amaretti cookies and 3–4 cherries. Fill the rest of each muffin cup with ice cream, pushing with the back of a spoon to disperse any air bubbles. Freeze for at least 6 hours or overnight, to set the ice cream solid.

Spread the almonds on a sheet of waxed paper. Dip the bottom of the muffin pan in warm water for about 10 seconds. Invert the ice-cream muffins onto the almonds and roll in the almonds to coat them entirely, pressing to make the nuts adhere. Set the tartuffi on a tray and refreeze until serving time. These can be made in advance and stored for 2–3 weeks. Fresh berries are a nice garnish.

Black Pepper & Ginger Pear Tart

I enjoyed a version of this tart in Italy with a glass of vin santo. Served at room temperature, the combination of fruit and spice is perfect with a dessert wine. Use a fine-quality peppercorn like Tellicherry or Malabar (available at specialty shops); the difference is amazing. It makes a deep 9- to 10-inch (23- to 25-cm) tart in a quiche or pie pan.

Serves 6 to 8		Glenys Morgan
1/2 cup	butter, chilled	120 mL
1 1/4 cups	flour	300 mL
1/2 tsp.	salt	2.5 mL
1/4 cup	cold water	60 mL
2	lemons, zest and juice	2
2 1/2 lbs.	ripe pears	1.1 kg
6–8 Tbsp.	sugar (adjust to the ripeness of the pears)	90–120 mL
3 Tbsp.	flour	45 mL
1 tsp.	black peppercorns	5 mL
1 Tbsp.	crystallized ginger, finely minced, or 1 tsp. (5 mL) ground ginger	15 mL
6 Tbsp.	sugar	90 mL
3 Tbsp.	flour	45 mL
1 Tbsp.	butter	15 mL

Cut the cold butter into 1/2-inch (1.2-cm) pieces. Combine the flour and salt. Add the butter pieces to the flour and blend, using a pastry blender or your fingertips to flatten the butter into pieces like large oatmeal flakes. Add the water and blend, shaping the dough into a ball. Wrap the ball in a piece of plastic wrap large enough to wrap generously around the dough. Flatten the dough inside the plastic into a disk approximately 1-inch (2.5-cm) thick. Chill for 30 minutes or longer before rolling.

Let the dough warm enough to roll without cracking. Roll to 1/8-inch (.3-cm) thickness and fit it into the pan. Prick the dough on the bottom of the pan with a fork. Trim the edges and chill until ready to use.

Preheat the oven to 450°F (230°C). Combine the lemon juice and zest in a large bowl. Place the juiced lemon halves in a large bowl of water. Peel, core and halve the pears, placing them in the bowl of water with the lemon halves as you work to prevent them from browning.

Cut the pears into bite-size pieces, adding them directly to the lemon juice and zest. Stir to coat the fruit. Combine the sugar and 3 Tbsp. (45 mL) flour in a small bowl. Use a mortar and pestle to crush the peppercorns or place them in a plastic bag and crush them with a rolling pin. Crushing produces less powder than grinding. Add the peppercorns to the sugar mixture. If using ground ginger rather than crystallized, add it to the sugar mixture as well.

Combine the lemon-coated pears with the sugar mixture, stirring to mix. Add the crystallized ginger. Pour the mixture into the prepared crust. Blend the remaining sugar, flour and butter together. Spread over the pears.

Place the tart in the preheated oven and bake for 15 minutes. Reduce the heat to 350°F (175°C) and bake until the crust is golden and the juices are bubbly and clear, 50–60 minutes. Cool at least 20 minutes before slicing.

Cabernet Cinnamon Pears with Mascarpone Surprise

I like to use Bosc pears because they have a great shape and long stems. Mascarpone cheese can be found in Italian grocery and specialty stores. Any good red wine could be substituted for Cabernet Sauvignon.

Serves 4		Mary Mackay
2 cups	Cabernet Sauvignon	475 mL
2	cinnamon sticks	2
3/4 cup	sugar	180 mL
4	firm pears with long stems	4
1/2 cup	mascarpone cheese	120 mL

In a medium pot bring the red wine, cinnamon sticks and sugar to a simmer. Peel the pears, leaving the stems intact. Use a melon baller to scoop the cores out of the pears and slice about 1/8 inch (.3 cm) off the bottoms so they will stand up. As each pear is done, drop it into the simmering syrup. Add enough water to allow the pears to float. Simmer until tender, about 40–70 minutes. To check for doneness, poke with the tip of a paring knife; the knife should glide through freely. Remove the pot from the heat and cool the pears to room temperature in the syrup. If desired, the pears can be left in the refrigerator overnight and finished the next day.

Remove the pears from the syrup and set aside. In a medium pot over high heat bring the syrup to a boil and reduce by half. Let cool.

Using a plain-tipped nozzle, fill a pastry bag with the mascarpone cheese and pipe the cheese inside the pears. To serve, place the stuffed pears on plates and drizzle a few tablespoons of syrup over each.

Fuji Brown Betty

Bettys are old desserts, and like many old things, shine when given some tender loving care. While seemingly utilitarian and frugal at first glance, Betty's beauty shines through when eaten. Crisp, buttered and sugared bread hides the tender, sweet and sour apples and soft, caramelized bottom. Fuji apples are a good choice because they become tender without getting mushy. For the bread, choose a loaf on the commercial side that still has a bit of integrity. Betty is best eaten the day she is baked.

Serves 6		Karen Barnaby
2 1/2 lbs.	Fuji apples, peeled, cored and halved	1.1 kg
1/2 cup	light brown sugar	120 mL
1 tsp.	ground cinnamon	5 mL
1/4 tsp.	ground cardamom	1.2 mL
	pinch salt	
1 Tbsp.	lemon juice	15 mL
2 Tbsp.	brandy	30 mL
2 Tbsp.	flour	30 mL
1	22- to 24-oz. (627- to 680-g) loaf of day-old white bread	1
1/2 cup	unsalted butter, melted	120 mL
1/2 cup	light brown sugar	120 mL
1/2 tsp.	cinnamon	2.5 mL

Preheat the oven to 325°F (165°C).

Cut the apples into 1/4-inch (.6-cm) slices. Place in a bowl and toss with 1/2 cup (120 mL) brown sugar, 1 tsp. (5 mL) cinnamon, cardamom, salt, lemon juice, brandy and flour.

Trim the crusts from the bread and cut into 1/2-inch (1.2-cm) cubes. Place in a large bowl and toss with the butter, sugar and cinnamon. Place half the bread cubes in an 8- x 11 1/2-inch (20- x 29-cm) glass baking dish. Spread the apple mixture on top and cover with the remaining bread cubes. Bake for 50–60 minutes, until the betty is well browned and caramelized on the bottom. Serve warm or at room temperature.

Valrhona Chocolate Bread Pudding with Crème Fraîche & Dried Cherry Port Sauce

If you are going to make and eat dessert, make it worth every bite. Valrhona 70% chocolate comes from France and has an amazingly smooth, intense, deep flavour. The 70% denotes the cocoa content in the chocolate. It is available in better-quality specialty food shops. Semisweet Belgian or Swiss can be substituted with good results.

Serves 8		Lesley Stowe
6	slices of brioche, challah or other egg bread, crusts removed	6
1/3 cup	unsalted butter, melted	80 mL
6 oz.	Valrhona chocolate, finely chopped	170 g
1 1/2 cups	whipping cream	360 mL
1/2 cup	milk	120 mL
6	egg yolks	6
1/3 cup	sugar	80 mL
2 Tbsp.	late-bottled vintage port	30 mL
4 oz.	Valrhona chocolate cut into 1/2-inch (1.2-cm) chunks	113 g
1/2 cup	dried cherries	120 mL
1/2 cup	port	120 mL
1/3 cup	sugar	80 mL
1 recipe	Crème Fraîche	1 recipe

Preheat the oven to 400°F (200°C). Lightly brush both sides of the bread slices with melted butter. Toast on a cookie sheet until golden brown.

Place the 6 oz. (170 g) chocolate in a saucepan with the cream and milk. Heat, stirring, until the chocolate is just melted. Whisk together the egg yolks, sugar and the 2 Tbsp. (30 mL) port. Whisk the chocolate cream into the yolk mixture.

Layer the toasted bread in a 10-inch (25-cm) buttered casserole dish. Sprinkle with the chocolate chunks. Pour the chocolate cream over the bread, cover and let stand for at least 1 hour, or refrigerate overnight.

Preheat the oven to 325°F (165°C). Set the casserole dish in a larger ovenproof pan. Add enough hot water to come halfway up the sides of the casserole dish. Bake for 1 hour. The top should be slightly set and custard-like.

While the pudding is baking, combine the cherries, the 1/2 cup (120 mL) port and sugar in a small saucepan. Simmer over low heat until the liquid becomes syrupy, approximately 10 minutes.

Remove the pudding from the water bath and serve while it is still warm with cherries and crème fraîche.

Crème Fraîche

Makes 1 cup (240 mL)

1 cup	whipping cream	240 mL
1 Tbsp.	buttermilk	15 mL

Mix together in a bowl and cover with plastic. Leave it at room temperature to thicken, 12–24 hours. Refrigerate until serving time.

White Chocolate Bread Pudding

A simple make-ahead dessert, comfort food at its finest. You can substitute almost any dried fruit for the cherries. I like it with a small amount of warm caramel sauce drizzled over the top.

Serves 8 to 10		Deb Connors
1/4 cup	melted butter	60 mL
1/2 cup	white sugar	120 mL
3	large eggs	3
3 Tbsp.	dark rum	45 mL
2 1/2 cups	heavy cream	600 mL
2	baguettes, cut in 1/2-inch (1.2-cm) slices, crust on	2
3/4 cup	grated white chocolate	180 mL
3/4 cup	tart dried cherries	180 mL
3 Tbsp.	light brown sugar	45 mL

Preheat the oven to 350°F (175°C). Lightly butter a 9- x 5-inch (23- x 12.5-cm) loaf pan and line the bottom with waxed paper.

In a large mixing bowl, whisk the melted butter and white sugar together. Beat in the eggs and rum until combined, then the heavy cream. Remove 1/2 cup (120 mL) and reserve. Add the baguette slices to the cream mixture and let sit for 5 minutes, stirring occasionally to make sure the bread is absorbing the cream. Squeeze the bread mixture by hand to break it up into pieces. Spread 1/3 of the bread mixture in a layer in the bottom of the prepared pan, pressing it down firmly. Sprinkle evenly with half the white chocolate and cherries. Cover with another 1/3 of the bread mixture, pressing down firmly. Sprinkle with the remaining white chocolate and cherries and finish with the remaining bread mixture. Press down firmly. Pour the reserved cream mixture over the top and sprinkle with brown sugar. Place the pudding in a larger pan filled with enough hot water to come halfway up the sides of the bread pan. Bake for 1 hour. Remove from the oven and cool on a rack for 1/2 hour.

If you wish to serve it in slices, let it cool in the pan for 2 more hours. At this time, loosen the pudding from the sides with a knife and turn out onto a cutting board. Remove the waxed paper and turn the pudding right side up. Slice it with a serrated knife and reheat on a baking sheet at 275°F (135°C) until warmed through, about 10 minutes.

Lemon, Fennel, Walnut & Sugar Loaf

I seldom feel that lemon sweet things are lemony enough and am always cramming more zest into them. This loaf is lemony enough and nicely balanced by the inherent sweetness of the fennel seeds.

Makes one 8 1/2- x 4 1/2-inch (21- x 11-cm) loaf		Karen Barnaby
2 1/4 cups	flour	535 mL
1 Tbsp.	baking powder	15 mL
1/4 tsp.	salt	1.2 mL
1 1/2 tsp.	fennel seeds, coarsely crushed	7.5 mL
4	lemons, zest only, finely chopped	4
3	eggs	3
2/3 cup	sugar	160 mL
1/3 cup	unsalted butter, melted	80 mL
1/2 cup	milk	120 mL
1 cup	coarsely chopped walnuts	240 mL
2 Tbsp.	sugar	30 mL

Preheat the oven to 350°F (175°C). Butter and flour an 8 1/2- x 4 1/2-inch (21- x 11-cm) loaf pan. Cut a piece of parchment paper to fit the bottom of the pan. Place it in the bottom of the pan and butter and flour the paper.

With a whisk, combine the flour, baking powder, salt, fennel seeds and lemon zest. In a large bowl, beat the eggs, 2/3 cup (160 mL) sugar and butter with an electric mixer for 2 minutes until light. Add the flour mixture and the milk alternately to the egg mixture in thirds, scraping down the sides of the bowl and beating only until combined. Fold in the walnuts. Scrape into the prepared pan and level the top. Sprinkle evenly with the 2 Tbsp. (30 mL) sugar.

Bake on the middle shelf of the oven for 50–60 minutes, until a cake tester comes out clean. Let cool in the pan on a rack for a few minutes, then loosen the sides and turn out onto the rack. Remove the parchment paper and turn right side up. Let cool completely before slicing.

Panforté di Sienna

This is my version of the delightful, firm fruitcake that has been made for centuries in Italy. It is wonderful served in small wedges for dessert. It is also a staple in my backpack when I go hiking or cross-country skiing. Purchasing fresh nuts is crucial to success. Making your own candied peel adds a very special taste, but you can use store-bought peel. Another key is making sure you bake it until just barely firm. Do not overbake.

Makes 32 small wedges		Margaret Chisholm
1 cup	honey	240 mL
3/4 cup	sugar	180 mL
1 cup	hazelnuts	240 mL
1 cup	almonds	240 mL
3/4 cup	finely chopped Candied Peel (recipe follows)	180 mL
2/3 cup	finely chopped dried apricot	160 mL
1/3 cup	raisins	80 mL
1/3 cup	currants or dried cherries	80 mL
1 1/2 cups	flour	360 mL
5 Tbsp.	cocoa powder	75 mL
1 Tbsp.	cinnamon	15 mL
1/2 tsp.	nutmeg	2.5 mL
1/8 tsp.	cloves	.5 mL
1/4 tsp.	mace	1.2 mL

Preheat the oven to 325°F (165°C).

Heat the honey and sugar together in a small saucepan over medium heat until the sugar is dissolved.

Combine all the other ingredients in a large bowl and stir well. Add the honey mixture and combine thoroughly. Using wet hands, spread the dough 1/2 inch (1.2 cm) thick on a 9- x 13-inch (23- x 33-cm) oiled or parchment-lined cookie sheet.

Bake until barely firm, approximately 18–20 minutes. Cool. Dust with icing sugar. Cut in small wedges.

Candied Peel

Makes 3/4 cup (180 mL)

3	medium oranges, peel only	3
1	lemon, peel only	1
3/4 cup	sugar	180 mL
2/3 cup	water	160 mL

Dice the orange and lemon peel into small pieces and simmer in a large pot of boiling water for 8 minutes. Drain, cool and chop. Place the sugar and water in a medium saucepan, bring to a boil and add the peel. Reduce to a simmer and cook for 25 minutes, or until the sugar syrup is very thick. Watch it carefully so it doesn't burn. Lift the peel onto a lightly buttered plate to cool. Discard the sugar syrup.

*B*lack Bottom Bourbon & Sour Cherry Cake

While Black Bottom Cake is not new, it should be remembered. I have updated it by adding bourbon and sour cherries, which combine marvelously with the chocolate and cream cheese. It is very easy to make and will keep for 5 days in the refrigerator if well wrapped.

Makes 1 10-inch (25-cm) tube pan		Karen Barnaby
1/2 cup	bourbon	120 mL
1 cup	dried sour cherries	240 mL
8 oz.	cream cheese	227 g
1/2 cup	sugar	120 mL
1	large egg	1
1 tsp.	pure vanilla extract	5 mL
12 oz.	bittersweet chocolate, chopped into 1/2-inch (1.2-cm) chunks	340 g
3 cups	all-purpose flour	720 mL
1/2 cup	cocoa powder	120 mL
2 tsp.	baking soda	10 mL
1/2 tsp.	salt	2.5 mL
2 cups	sugar	475 mL
2/3 cup	vegetable oil	160 mL
2	large eggs	2
1 cup	water	240 mL
1 cup	milk	240 mL
1 Tbsp.	white vinegar	15 mL
1 tsp.	pure vanilla extract	5 mL

In a small pot, gently warm the bourbon. Add the cherries. Simmer for a minute, then remove from the heat. Let cool completely.

With a hand mixer or by hand, cream the cream cheese. Gradually add the 1/2 cup (120 mL) sugar. Beat in the egg and vanilla, scraping down the sides of the bowl. Stir in the bourbon-soaked cherries, any bourbon left in the pot and the chocolate chunks. Set aside.

Preheat the oven to 350°F (175°C).

In a large bowl, sift the flour, cocoa, baking soda, salt and sugar together. In a separate bowl, either by hand or with an electric mixer, beat the oil, eggs, water, milk, vinegar and vanilla until well mixed. Combine with the dry ingredients and beat until smooth, scraping down the sides of the bowl.

Pour half the batter into a well-buttered and floured 10-inch (25-cm) tube pan. Spoon the cream cheese mixture evenly over the batter. Pour the remaining batter over the cream cheese and smooth the top.

Bake on the middle shelf for 1 1/4–1 1/2 hours, or until a cake tester comes out clean. Let cool on a rack for 10 minutes. Run a spatula around the outside of the pan to loosen it, then turn out of the pan onto the rack. Let cool completely before cutting.

Angel Food Cake with Fresh Berries & Orange Crème Anglaise

An old-time favourite, a perfect summer dessert. Use your favourite fresh berries and serve it in the garden.

Serves 8 to 10		Deb Connors
1 cup	cake flour, sifted	240 mL
1 1/2 cups	sugar	360 mL
1 1/2 cups	egg whites at room temperature	360 mL
1 1/4 tsp.	cream of tartar	6.2 mL
1/8 tsp.	salt	.5 mL
1/2 tsp.	vanilla extract	2.5 mL
3 Tbsp.	finely chopped orange zest	45 mL
2 tsp.	fresh orange juice	10 mL
	fresh berries of your choice	
1 recipe	Orange Crème Anglaise	1 recipe
	sprigs of mint or lemon balm	

Preheat the oven to 375°F (190°C). Sift the flour with 1/2 cup (120 mL) of the sugar and set aside.

With an electric mixer or food processor, whip the egg whites until foamy. Add the cream of tartar and salt and continue whipping until soft peaks form. Continue whipping. Add the remaining sugar slowly in a thin stream and whip until stiff and glossy.

Working quickly, using a rubber spatula, fold in the reserved flour-sugar mixture, vanilla, orange zest and juice. Gently spoon the batter into an ungreased 10-inch (25-cm) tube pan. Bake 30 to 35 minutes until golden brown. A skewer inserted into the centre of the cake should come out clean. Turn the cake pan upside down on the neck of a wine bottle and let cool.

Slide a knife around the inside edge of the pan. Place a serving plate on top of the cake and turn it upside down. Shake the cake out onto the plate. Turn the cake right side up.

To serve, top each slice with fresh berries, pour anglaise over top and garnish with mint or lemon balm.

Orange Crème Anglaise

1/2 cup	milk	120 mL
1/2 cup	cream	120 mL
1/2	vanilla bean	1/2
1	orange, zest only	1
4	large egg yolks	4
3 Tbsp.	sugar	45 mL
	pinch salt	

In a heavy saucepan combine the milk, cream, vanilla bean and orange zest. Scald over medium-high heat. Let cool 5 minutes and strain. Whisk together the egg yolks, sugar and salt for 2 minutes. Whisk the strained cream into the egg yolks. Put the bowl over a pot of simmering water and stir the mixture with a wooden spoon until it starts to thicken, about 5 minutes. It should coat the back of the spoon. Chill.

Caramelized Pear Ginger Upside-Down Cake with Poire William Nutmeg Cream

Next to chocolate, desserts involving caramel are my favourite. Served warm with the Poire William Nutmeg Cream, this is an elegant pudding, as the English would describe it.

Serves 8		Lesley Stowe
2 1/2 lbs.	pears, ripe but not soft, about 10	1.1 kg
1/2 cup	unsalted butter	120 mL
1 1/2 cups	sugar	360 mL
3/4 cup	unsalted butter	180 mL
4 Tbsp.	brown sugar	60 mL
4	egg yolks	4
1/2 cup	molasses	120 mL
2 cups	flour	475 mL
2 Tbsp.	ground ginger	30 mL
2 tsp.	cinnamon	10 mL
1/2 tsp.	nutmeg	2.5 mL
1/2 tsp.	ground cloves	2.5 mL
2 tsp.	baking soda	10 mL
4 Tbsp.	strong hot coffee	60 mL
8	egg whites	8
4 Tbsp.	sugar	60 mL
1 recipe	Poire William Nutmeg Cream	1 recipe

Peel and core the pears. Cut in half lengthwise.

In a heavy-bottomed sauté pan melt the 1/2 cup (120 mL) butter and sugar. Cook over low heat until the mixture caramelizes, 10–15 minutes. Do not stir the mixture as it will start to crystallize. You don't want the caramel to get too dark. Remove from the heat and add the pears. Cook until the pears are thoroughly caramelized, 15–20 minutes, turning them over halfway through. When cooked through, you should be able to easily pierce them with a knife. Remove from the heat, drain off all the caramel and reserve. Arrange the pears in a decorative pattern in the bottom of a 10-inch (25-cm) pan, with the cut side facing up.

Preheat the oven to 350°F (175°C). Beat the 3/4 cup (180 mL) butter until it holds soft peaks; beat in the brown sugar. In a small bowl stir together the egg yolks and molasses. Combine the flour, ginger, cinnamon, nutmeg and cloves. Beating at low speed, add the dry ingredients and the egg yolk mixture alternately to the butter mixture, beginning and ending with dry ingredients. Just before adding the last portion of dry ingredients, dissolve the baking soda in the coffee and beat it in. Whisk the whites, add the 4 Tbsp. (60 mL) sugar, and whisk until soft peaks form. Add 1/3 of the egg whites to the batter and stir. Gently fold in the remaining egg whites.

Pour the batter on top of the caramelized pears. Bake for 45–55 minutes. The top should be shiny and firm. Let cool 15 minutes before turning it out onto a plate. To serve, drizzle each plate with the reserved caramel. Place a slice of cake on top of the caramel and spoon the cream on the side.

Poire William Nutmeg Cream

Makes 2 1/2 cups (600 mL)

1 1/2 cups	heavy cream	360 mL
2 Tbsp.	granulated sugar	30 mL
1/4 tsp.	nutmeg	1.2 mL
4 Tbsp.	Poire William or pear liqueur	60 mL

Beat the cream and sugar for 2–5 minutes, or until it forms soft peaks. Fold in the nutmeg and Poire William. Chill until ready to serve.

Chocolate Walnut Torte with "Tiramisu" Cream

Fresh, high-quality walnuts are essential for this dish. Try purchasing them at a busy health food store or specialty nut shop.

Serves 12		Margaret Chisholm
1/2 lb.	bittersweet chocolate, chopped	225 g
1 1/2 cups	walnuts	360 mL
1/3 cup	all-purpose flour	80 mL
1/2 cup	unsalted butter, softened to room temperature	120 mL
1/2 cup	sugar	120 mL
7	eggs, separated	7
1/8 tsp.	salt	.5 mL
1/8 tsp.	cream of tartar	.5 mL
6 Tbsp.	sugar	90 mL
	cocoa powder for dusting	
1 recipe	"Tiramisu" Cream	1 recipe

Preheat the oven to 350°F (175 °C). Grease the sides and bottom of a 9-inch (23-cm) springform pan.

Place the chocolate in a heatproof bowl over a simmering pot of water. Stir occasionally until melted. Set aside to cool for 5 minutes. Process the walnuts and flour in a food processor or blender until the mixture resembles bread crumbs.

Beat the butter and the 1/2 cup (120 mL) sugar in an electric mixer until light and fluffy. Beat in the melted chocolate. Add the egg yolks one at a time and beat for 3 more minutes. Fold in the walnut mixture.

Beat the egg whites with the salt and cream of tartar to firm peaks. Continue beating while gradually adding the remaining sugar. Fold the egg whites into the chocolate mixture.

Pour into the prepared pan and bake for 50–60 minutes. Let sit for 10 minutes before removing. Cool. Dust with cocoa and serve with "Tiramisu" Cream.

"Tiramisu" Cream

Makes 1 1/3 cups (320 mL)

This very simple topping has the fabulous flavours of the wildy popular Tiramisu without all of the work.

1/2 lb.	mascarpone cheese	225 g
2 Tbsp.	brewed espresso	30 mL
2 Tbsp.	sugar	30 mL
2 Tbsp.	brandy	30 mL

Stir all the ingredients together in a bowl. Chill until ready to use.

Warm Apple Crumb Cake

This must be one of the first cakes I learned how to make as a little girl. I have been making it ever since, because it's delicious and very easy. You can use plums or good-quality canned peaches instead of the apples. Serve it warm with whipped cream or ice cream.

Makes one 9-inch (23-cm) cake		Tamara Kourchenko
2 lbs.	apples, peeled, cored and quartered	900 g
1 cup	light brown sugar	240 mL
1	4-inch (10-cm) cinnamon stick	1
2 cups	water	475 mL
3 cups	flour	720 mL
1/2 cup	sugar	120 mL
1 tsp.	baking powder	5 mL
2	large eggs	2
2 tsp.	vanilla extract	10 mL
1 tsp.	ground cinnamon	5 mL
1 tsp.	ground nutmeg	5 mL
1 cup	butter, cut in 1/2-inch (1.2-cm) pieces	240 mL

Preheat the oven to 350°F (175°C). Butter a 9-inch (23-cm) springform pan.

Place the apples, sugar, cinnamon stick and water in a pot. Bring to a boil and simmer until the apples are soft, about 20 minutes. Let the apples cool in the liquid.

Combine the flour, sugar, baking powder, eggs, vanilla, cinnamon and nutmeg in a food processor. Pulse briefly to mix well. Start the motor, and with the motor running, add the pieces of butter one at a time. Process until it resembles coarse meal and the mix starts to hold together.

Press half the crumb mixture on the bottom and 1/2 inch (1.2 cm) up the sides of the cake pan. Drain the apples and spread on the cake. Sprinkle the rest of the crumb mixture evenly over the apples, pressing some of the mix a little with your fingers to form bigger crumbs.

Bake for about 45 minutes or until the larger crumbs turn golden brown. Serve warm with ice cream or whipped cream.

Chai-Spiced Butter Balls

Tearoom T has been an inspiration for me since they invited me for a tea-tasting several years ago. I recall only sampling 27, and was told that the record was 40! I've used their tea as a marinade for salmon and goat's cheese and dabbled with it in baking. This was my most successful cookie experiment and would make a fantastic Christmas cookie.

Makes 30 cookies		Karen Barnaby
2 1/4 cups	flour, sifted	535 mL
1/2 tsp.	salt	2.5 mL
1 Tbsp.	Herbal Spice Chai, sifted	15 mL
1 cup	unsalted butter, at room temperature	240 mL
1/4 cup	icing sugar, sifted	60 mL
1 tsp.	vanilla	5 mL
1–1 1/2 cups	icing sugar, for rolling the cookies in	240–360 mL

Preheat the oven to 400°F (200°C).

Combine the flour, salt and chai with a whisk until well mixed. In a large bowl, beat the butter with an electric mixer until smooth. Gradually beat in the 1/4 cup (60 mL) icing sugar and the vanilla until fluffy. Add the dry ingredients and mix only until combined. The dough will be a bit crumbly.

Roll level tablespoons of dough into balls and place 1 inch (2.5 cm) apart on parchment-lined baking sheets. Bake in the middle of the oven for 10 minutes, until lightly golden and pale brown on the bottoms. Let cool on the pan for 5 minutes on a cooling rack.

Place the icing sugar in a shallow container and roll each cookie in the sugar, covering it completely. Transfer to a rack to cool. When completely cooled, roll in the icing sugar again. Store in an airtight container between layers of waxed or parchment paper.

Margaret Chisholm

I was born in Montreal into a family that hails from the great food-loving traditions of the Maritimes. My grandmother Margaret Chisholm senior owned and operated Peggy's Lunch, a café in Nova Scotia, and taught me the value of butter. Grandmother Alvina was born in Oyster Bed Bridge, Prince Edward Island, and taught me the value of oysters.

I started cooking at a very young age and was a veritable gourmet by my teen years. Being in a large family gave me an instant critical audience. I wrote my first recipe for "Spaghetti à la Margaret" at age fifteen. My older brother said it was awful.

My first serious cooking job was at Skoki Lodge in the Canadian Rockies, eight miles from the nearest road catering to skiers and hikers. There I learned to cook dinner for thirty on a wood stove. After ten years of cooking adventures in locations throughout western Canada, from ski lodges to fishing and gold-mining camps, I decided to make it my career.

I trained at Peter Kump's New York Cooking School, where I received a blue ribbon diploma. I apprenticed with Anne Rosensweig at Manhattan's Arcadia Restaurant. Living in the food world of New York City had an enormous impact on me. I returned to Vancouver determined to contribute to raising the level of awareness in the area of fine food and wine.

Since settling in Vancouver twelve years ago I have been a caterer, a cooking teacher and cookbook writer.

I developed and taught Cooking Classes for the Serious Amateur at the Dubrulle French Culinary School. That five-year period was very rewarding both professionally and personally. Being a teacher demanded that I increase my level of knowledge and hone my skills; it was also a lot of fun. I continue to teach a few classes in Vancouver and Calgary.

I have returned to the fabulous world of catering and am currently executive chef at Culinary Capers Catering in Vancouver. An experienced full service caterer, we cater to a complete range of clients, from a picnic for two to a dinner for thousands.

Grandmother Margaret Chisholm's Coconut Oatmeal Cookies

Both of my grandmothers were fabulous cooks. My grandmother Margaret won a local newspaper contest with this delicious buttery cookie. I grew up with margarine in the house except for one week a year, in August, when she would visit and my parents would spring for a costly pound of butter.

Makes 3 dozen cookies		*Margaret Chisholm*
1 1/2 cups	all-purpose flour	360 mL
1 tsp.	baking powder	5 mL
1 tsp.	baking soda	5 mL
1/2 tsp.	salt	2.5 mL
1 1/2 cups	rolled oats	360 mL
3/4 cup	coconut	180 mL
1 cup	butter	240 mL
3/4 cup	brown sugar	180 mL
3/4 cup	white sugar	180 mL
1	egg	1
1 tsp.	vanilla	5 mL

Preheat the oven to 325°F (165°C). Grease a cookie sheet.

Sift together the flour, baking powder, baking soda and salt. Stir in the oats and coconut. Set aside.

Beat the butter until soft and creamy. Beat in the sugars, then the egg and vanilla. Continue to beat until smooth and light. Combine the butter mixture with the flour mixture and stir until just combined.

Drop the cookie mixture by tablespoonfuls onto the cookie sheet. Press flat with a fork. Bake for approximately 15 minutes, or until lightly brown and the centres are barely firm. Cool on a rack.

Sun-Dried Berry & Chocolate Bars

A good-quality Dutch-process cocoa makes this dark and rich.
The sun-dried berries keep it moist for days so it's excellent to
take on a picnic or away for the weekend. The addition of
pepper or crushed chiles takes it to another level and while there,
enjoy with a glass of Quady Black Muscat Elyssium.

Makes one 8-inch (20-cm) square pan		Glenys Morgan
2/3 cup	unsalted butter	160 mL
1 cup	dark brown sugar, firmly packed	240 mL
6 Tbsp.	cocoa powder, preferably Dutch-process (such as Bendsorp, Droeste or Valrhona)	90 mL
1 tsp.	vanilla	5 mL
2	large eggs	2
1/2 cup	flour	120 mL
1/2 cup	sun-dried berries—blueberries, cranberries, cherries, or a mixture	120 mL
1/2 tsp.	cinnamon	2.5 mL
1 Tbsp.	instant coffee granules (optional)	15 mL
1/4 tsp.	crushed red chiles or black pepper (optional)	1.2 mL

Preheat the oven to 325°F (165°C). Melt the butter and sugar together. Blend in the cocoa and vanilla, beating until glossy. Stir in the eggs, one at a time. Add the flour, mixing well. Fold in the sun-dried berries, cinnamon, coffee and if desired, the chiles or pepper.

Lightly grease an 8-inch (20-cm) square pan. Spread the batter evenly in the pan. Oiling or spraying the spatula with vegetable spray helps to spread the batter easily. Bake for 30–35 minutes. The cake should be firm but not dry. Cool before cutting. Cut into triangles or pie-shaped wedges for an interesting presentation. If desired, serve with Deep Dark Chocolate Sauce.

Deep Dark Chocolate Sauce

3/4 cup	sifted cocoa powder, preferably Dutch-process	180 mL
3/4 cup	sugar	180 mL
	pinch salt	
1 cup	cold water	240 mL
2 Tbsp.	unsalted butter	30 mL

In a saucepan, combine the cocoa, sugar and salt. Add the water and whisk until smooth. Over moderate heat, bring to a low boil. Simmer for 3–4 minutes and stir in the butter. Simmer for 3–4 minutes longer. Slow cooking will reduce the sauce to a very thick consistency. Refrigerate in a sealed jar or microwaveable container for easy warming.

Double Chocolate & Ginger Biscotti

Chocolate and ginger has been a long-time favourite combination of mine. I usually satisfy my taste buds by eating chocolate-covered ginger, but these are deep, rich and chocolatey and do an excellent job.

Makes approximately 45 biscotti		Karen Barnaby
2 2/3 cups	flour	640 mL
1 cup	cocoa powder	240 mL
1 1/2 tsp.	baking soda	7.5 mL
1/4 tsp.	salt	1.2 mL
1 cup	granulated sugar	240 mL
1 cup	light brown sugar	240 mL
8 oz.	good-quality bittersweet chocolate, finely chopped	225 g
3/4 cup	unsalted butter, at room temperature	180 mL
3	large eggs	3
1 tsp.	vanilla	5 mL
1/2 cup	crystallized ginger, chopped into irregular-sized pieces from 1/4 inch (.6 cm) to 1/2 inch (1.2 cm)	120 mL

Preheat the oven to 325°F (165°C). Combine the flour, cocoa, baking soda, salt and sugars in a large bowl. Whisk until well mixed.

Place 1 cup (240 mL) of the mixture and the chocolate in the workbowl of a food processor. Pulse until the chocolate is finely ground. Mix into the dry mixture. Add the butter and mix with an electric mixer or your fingertips to a fine mealy texture.

Beat the eggs and vanilla together. Add to the flour mixture along with the ginger and stir or beat until well combined. The dough will be soft.

Shape into three 15-inch (38-cm) logs and transfer to 3 parchment-lined baking sheets. The dough will spread quite a bit while baking. Bake on the middle shelf of the oven for 30–40 minutes, until the sides are firm and the tops are cracked. Place the pan on a cooling rack and let cool until firm enough to handle. Transfer to a cutting surface and cut with a serrated knife into 1/2-inch (1.2-cm) slices.

Reduce the oven temperature to 300°F (150°C). Return the cookies to the baking sheet and bake for 15 minutes, until dry. The biscotti will crisp as they cool. Cool completely and store between layers of waxed or parchment paper in an airtight container.

West Coast Fruit & Nut Cookies

Cookies, whether you are young or old, are comfort food. We can always use another cookie recipe, especially when they taste like these.

Makes about 24 cookies		Caren McSherry-Valagao
1/4 lb.	unsalted butter	113 g
1/3 cup	brown sugar	80 mL
1	large egg	1
1 tsp.	pure vanilla extract	5 mL
3/4 cup	unbleached all-purpose flour	180 mL
1/2 tsp.	baking powder	2.5 mL
1/2 tsp.	sea salt	2.5 mL
1/2 cup	chopped toasted hazelnuts	120 mL
1/4 cup	rolled oats	60 mL
1/4 cup	sun-dried cranberries	60 mL
1/4 cup	sun-dried blueberries	60 mL
1/4 cup	sun-dried cherries	60 mL
1/2 cup	chopped semisweet good chocolate	120 mL

Preheat the oven to 350°F (175°C). Cream the butter. Add the sugar and beat until the mixture is light and fluffy, about 5 minutes. Beat in the egg and vanilla.

Sift the flour, baking powder and salt together. Mix it into the batter along with the nuts, oats, dried fruit and chocolate. Stir the batter to combine.

Using an ice cream scoop (to make the cookies all uniform in size), scoop onto greased cookie sheets, spacing 1–2 inches (2.5–5 cm) apart, and bake for 15–20 minutes, or until light golden brown.

Crème Unbrûléed

A classic crème brûlée with a hard chocolate topping instead of burnt sugar. Ideal for the majority of households lacking the welding equipment to get a proper flame-burned topping.

Serves 4		Mary Mackay
2 cups	whipping cream	475 mL
5	egg yolks	5
1/4 cup	sugar	60 mL
1/2 tsp.	pure vanilla extract	2.5 mL
	pinch salt	
1 oz.	bittersweet chocolate, finely chopped	28 g

Preheat the oven to 325°F (165°C).

Heat the whipping cream in a pot over medium-high heat until small bubbles appear around the edges. Whisk the egg yolks in a bowl until pale yellow. Continue whisking and add the sugar in a slow steady stream. Slowly whisk in the warm cream 1 Tbsp. (15 mL) at a time. Add the vanilla and salt. Strain the mixture through a sieve.

Place four 1/2-cup (120-mL) ramekins into a baking dish. Pour the mixture into the ramekins. Pour warm water into the baking dish, to come halfway up the ramekins, and cover the dish with foil. Bake until just set—the custard should wobble a little in the middle—about 35–45 minutes. Remove the dish from the oven and let the ramekins cool in the water bath. Remove from the water bath and cover with plastic wrap. Refrigerate at least 2 hours and up to 1 day.

For the chocolate topping, heat a small pot of water until just simmering, then remove from the heat. Place half the finely chopped chocolate into a bowl and set on top of the warm water, without touching the water. Stir the chocolate until melted. Remove the bowl from the heat, add the remaining chocolate and stir until melted. Working with one ramekin at a time, spread a thin layer of chocolate over the tops of the custards (the back of a teaspoon works well). Alternatively, the melted chocolate can be placed in a pastry bag and piped on top of the custards. Put the custards back into the refrigerator for about 5 minutes, then serve.

Orange Maple Crème Brûlée

Rich, elegant and simple. It's worth tracking down the vanilla bean for this dessert. The real thing tastes so much better. Do not be alarmed at the little black specks floating in your brûlée mixture. They are the seeds from the vanilla pod. You can make this dessert the day before, cover the ramekins tightly with plastic wrap and refrigerate. Be very careful when removing the water bath from the oven.

Serves 6		Deb Connors
3 Tbsp.	maple syrup	45 mL
2/3 cup	milk	160 mL
2 cups	heavy cream	475 mL
1/2	vanilla bean, split lengthwise	1/2
3	oranges, zest only, finely chopped	3
6	large egg yolks	6
1/2 cup	white sugar	120 mL
6 Tbsp.	white sugar	90 mL

Preheat the oven to 350°F (175°C).

In a heavy-bottomed medium saucepan combine the maple syrup, milk, cream, vanilla bean and orange zest. Scald the mixture over medium-high heat. In a medium bowl whisk together the egg yolks and 1/2 cup (120 mL) sugar. Whisk the scalded cream into the egg yolk mixture. Refrigerate until cool and strain. Pour the mixture into six 6-oz. (170-mL) ramekins. Place the ramekins in a baking pan and put it in the oven. Fill the pan with hot water until it is halfway up the sides of the ramekins. Cover the pan with foil. Bake 45–50 minutes, until the custard is set except for a small area in the centre. Remove the ramekins from the water and let them cool. Cover each custard with plastic wrap and refrigerate for several hours or overnight.

To serve, preheat the boiler. Sprinkle each custard evenly with 1 Tbsp. (15 mL) white sugar. Place the custards on a rack approximately 3–4 inches (8–10 cm) from the broiler until the sugar is caramelized, 1–3 minutes. Watch carefully to make sure the custards don't burn.

Allow the caramelized sugar to cool for a few moments and serve.

Maple Crème Brûlée with Cherries

I am a total fanatic when it comes to Crème Brûlée. I love the creamy consistency that contrasts with the crunchy caramel. The easiest way to caramelize them is with a torch (available in most hardware stores). If you don't feel comfortable using a torch, a very hot broiler works too. Just make sure not to heat the custard too much. Some kitchen stores also sell irons specially designed for this job.

Serves 8		Tamara Kourchenko
3/4 cup	pure maple syrup	180 mL
4	large egg yolks	4
2	large eggs	2
2 1/4 cups	whipping cream	535 mL
3/4 cup	whole milk	180 mL
2 Tbsp.	Irish cream liqueur (such as Bailey's)	30 mL
1	10-oz. (284-mL) can cherries in water, pitted and drained	1
6 Tbsp.	granulated sugar	90 mL

Preheat the oven to 300°F (150°C).

In a large bowl, whisk together the maple syrup, egg yolks and eggs. Combine the cream and milk and bring to a boil in a heavy saucepan. Remove from the heat and, whisking constantly, gradually add the cream mixture to the egg mixture. Whisk in the liqueur.

Place six 6-oz. (170-mL) ramekins or custard cups in a baking pan. Divide the cherries among the containers and fill with the custard. Pour enough hot water into the pan to reach halfway up the sides of the containers. Bake until set, about 1 hour. Refrigerate overnight.

Just before serving, sprinkle 1 Tbsp. (15 mL) sugar evenly on each custard and caramelize with a torch, or place under a hot broiler until the sugar melts.

Lemon Crème Brûlée Imposters

Julia Child may use a blowtorch but this version browns itself in the oven. This is not a purist's crème brûlée, but it's hard to resist what's below the cloud-like top. The herb-flavoured variation is refreshing, but so is plain lemon.

Serves 4 to 6 generously		Glenys Morgan
1 1/2 cups	milk	360 mL
1	sprig fresh rosemary or mint (optional)	1
4	large eggs, separated	4
1/4 cup	unsalted butter, softened	60 mL
1 cup	granulated sugar	240 mL
2–3	lemons, zest and 1/2 cup (120 mL) juice	2–3
1/4 cup	flour	60 mL

For the herb-infused version, scald the milk and herb sprig together in a small saucepan. Remove from the heat and let the milk cool. Strain and proceed with the recipe. For plain lemon, omit this step.

Preheat the oven to 375°F (190°C). With a whisk or beater, beat the egg whites until stiff and glossy. Use the same whisk and a new bowl to cream the butter, sugar, egg yolks and lemon zest. Beat until the sugar dissolves. Stir in the flour and mix well. Stir in the milk and lemon juice. Don't worry if it looks curdled. Fold the beaten egg whites through the lemon mixture.

Pour the mixture into a 1-quart (1-L) gratin or pie dish. For individual servings, use ramekins or custard cups instead. Place the gratin dish or ramekins in a pan large enough to hold them—a lasagna dish works well. Pour in very hot water until it reaches halfway up the side of the filled gratin dish or ramekins. Bake for 30 minutes and check for brown tops on the custard. Place a piece of foil over top and bake another 15 minutes. Individual ramekins will finish cooking in about 30–35 minutes. Cool slightly or to room temperature and serve.

Index